Foreword

As Minister for Children I am delighted to publish 'fathers and families: research and reflection on key questions'. This is the third report to be published by the Department of Health and Children under the Springboard Initiative. It is written to promote understanding and appreciation of the role of a fathers in family life.

In traditional families, fathers had a clear role as the family patriarch. He was head of the family, its protector and the person who provided for the families material needs. With the increased participation of mothers in the labour force and the growing number of one parent households, fathers are no longer the exclusive providers. These changes have confronted fathers with the need to redefine their role and function within the family and, in particular, their role as parents.

A key theme which informs this report is that no one should be left out of the family picture. An inclusive society requires an inclusive family. Mothers, fathers and children, including the extended family, are all part of the family picture which, for all the difficulties of family life, is part of the reality to which everyone belongs. This report is part of the process of keeping fathers in the family picture alongside mothers and children and, as such, is based on the belief that an inclusive family helps to create an inclusive society. "Ní neart go cur le chéile".

The development of services for fathers faces a number of specific challenges including: finding out the needs of fathers, particularly the needs of different types of vulnerable fathers; adopting and promoting a strengths based perspective to work with fathers as with families generally; training professionals to see fathers as part of the family even where they are not living in the same household as the mother and child; recruiting more men in to the caring professionals and promoting awareness of family services in a way which is seen as supportive of men and fathers at every stage of the life cycle from child birth to old age.

I appreciate that fathers involvement in quality parenting is important for the development and well-being of their children and their participation in this parenting can contribute to increased parental equality, both within and outside the home. Through its Family Support Projects the Springboard Family Support Initiative will continue to try to engage with these vulnerable fathers.

Mary Hanafin

Mary Hanafin T.D.
Minister for Children

TABLE OF CONTENTS

Structure of Report

"Fathers and families need new images of what a father can be, images that go beyond the idea of father as outsider, father as provider, or father as intruder in the home. There is a need for images that acknowledge father as a potent nurturant force within the family as well as a creative liaison with the world outside the family"

ARTHUR COLMAN AND LIBBY COLMAN, 1988:1-2.

This report is based on a reflective reading of the now extensive body of research which has accumulated on the theme of fathers over the past decade or so. In this sense, the report is built on a solid foundation of research evidence. However facts need to be interpreted and the report tries to reflect upon the significance of this research, particularly in the context of Irish fathers and families.

Each chapter in the report addresses a key question about fathers. This format seems most appropriate in terms of focusing attention on the central issues of fact and interpretation which need to be clarified. In addition, this approach is designed to make the report as accessible as possible to the growing number of people who, in addition to their own personal interest in fathers and families, also have an ongoing professional interest in them as well. The nine key questions which are addressed in the report are:

- Why a report on fathers?
- Is the role of fathers changing?
- How are men initiated into fatherhood?
- What impact do fathers have on children?
- How does the law treat fathers?
- How do non-resident fathers parent their children?
- How do stepfathers parent their children?
- How can family services support fathers?
- Can fathering skills be taught?

This report is written to promote understanding and appreciation of the role of fathers in family life. It is curious that such a report needs to be written but the evidence in the report itself will show that it does. One of Ireland's leading clinical psychologists who has spent a lifetime working with troubled families and children, when invited to reflect on his concerns and hopes for children in the new millennium, wrote: "First concern: the retreat of the father in Ireland as in the western world. My corresponding hope is that men will figure more and more centrally in families. ... Does anyone really believe that children are better off without a father? ... If we seek a better deal for every Irish child in the third millennium, the difference will be found largely in the quality of fathering"[1].

In Ireland, as in the rest of the Western world, the public image of fathers is laced with ambiguity and uncertainty. There is, for example, the contrast between traditional and modern fathers. The "traditional" father is seen as a hard working breadwinner but is often absent, both physically and emotionally, from his children. The "modern" father is seen as pushing prams and changing nappies, taking children to school and playing with them in the park, etc. There are also images of the father which depict both positive and negative qualities[2]. There are loving fathers, dependable fathers, involved fathers, committed fathers, strong fathers, adoring fathers but equally, there are disinterested fathers, unreliable fathers, workaholic fathers, abusive fathers, weak fathers, violent fathers, absent fathers. This kaleidoscopic imagery of fatherhood stands in contrast to the public imagery associated with motherhood which tends to be consistently positive – although that too can carry a hidden burden[3].

Fathers are now being judged against changing expectations of what it is to be a good fathers. Good fathers are increasingly expected, and expect themselves, to be emotionally involved with their children, in addition to being a good provider. They usually expect and are expected to share housework and take an interest in the children's schooling. It is no longer presumed that the father is the sole breadwinner or that his role is simply to supply the weekly wage packet. There is a presumption that fathers will want to be at the birth of their children – which nine out of ten are[4] - and that they will have the same practical skills of child rearing - apart from breast-feeding - as the mother. Few contemporary fathers have actually experienced this type of fathering themselves. As a result, many of them cannot rely on their own fathers as models of good fathers, even if they were good fathers by the standards of their time.

Why a Report on Fathers?

"The paternal presence is a vital, life-giving force in the lives of children and families. Although we have made some progress in understanding the impact of paternal absence on children, we must now begin to understand, define and appreciate the meaning of paternal presence".

KYLE D. PRUETT, 1993:50.

---

1 Andrews, 2000. Paul Andrews, SJ is a child psychologist in private practice and former Director of St. Declan's Child Guidance Clinic. He is the author of the book Changing Children: Living with a New Generation (Andrews, 1994) as well as numerous articles.

2 A number of writers have commented on the public image of fathers, and its frequently negative connotations (see for example Hillman, 1996:80; Burgess, 1997:19-20; Bradshaw, Stimson, Skinner and Williams, 1999b:405; Clare, 2000:158). In Ireland, the Exploring Masculinities Programme, a programme for young boys in Irish secondary schools, is heavily influenced by negative images of men and fathers which, however unwittingly, typically deplore rather than explore masculinities (see Department of Education and Science, 2000).

3 Featherstone and Holloway, 1997

4 Lewis and Warin, 2001:3.

Despite the changes affecting fatherhood, it is still the case that, on average, fathers do more paid work than mothers just as mothers do more childcare and housework than fathers. This asymmetry is amply illustrated in Table 1.1 which shows that, among a random sample of married couples in six urban areas in the UK in 1987, women do an average of about two thirds of all unpaid work in the home while, on average, men do about two thirds of all paid work outside the home.

Table 1.1 Sharing of Paid and Unpaid Work Among UK Couples in 1987

Category	Unpaid Work* Hours Per Day	%	Paid Work Hours Per Day	%	Total Hours Per Day	%
Wives	6.9	68	2.2	31	9.1	53
Husbands	3.3	32	4.8	69	8.1	47
Total	10.2	100	7.0	100	17.2	100

* This refers to all household activities, including childcare and housework.

Source: Layte, 1999, Chapter Two. The data is from the UK's Social Change in Economic Life Survey (SCELI) carried out at the University of Essex and is based on an achieved random sample of 387 UK couples – excluding ethnic minorities – where a separate time use diary was kept by the husband and wife over a seven day period in 1987.

"You can't have a father without a child; you can't have a child without a father"

REB ANDERSON, 1998:144.

These statistics, which are in line with other research on this topic[5], need to be seen in the broader historical context that, on average, fathers do more childcare and housework than fathers in previous generations. According to one review of the British evidence: "surveys show that fathers' involvement in the home has been increasing and the 'gender gap' in terms of average time spent caring for children has narrowed. Fathers in many homes are reported to play a central role as playmates for younger children and as organisers of family activities. Interviews with the 33-year old parents who were part of the NCDS [National Child Development Study which started in 1958] found that fathers who were actively involved in childcare were also more likely to play out of doors with their children"[6]. A similar picture emerges from US research on the division of labour between men and women in the home: "in effect, the household gap is closing not just because fathers are doing more at home, but because mothers are doing more in the workplace and less at home. But combined with the added hours that fathers continue to spend at their paid work, the total number of hours that mothers and fathers spend providing for and caring for their families is converging"[7].

---

[5] For reviews, see Ferri and Smith, 1996, Chapter Three; Burghes, Clarke and Cronin, 1997, Chapter Five.
[6] Lewis, 2000:3.
[7] Levine and Pittinsky, 1997:26.

In Ireland the only study on the domestic division of labour – based on interviews in the late 1980s with mothers only, a risky methodological procedure given that research involving couples is fraught with the difficulty that men and women in the same relationship perceive themselves and their contribution to the family differently[8] – found that women did much more housework and childcare than men but also found that the majority of women (70%) were satisfied with this arrangement[9]. More recent research in Ireland suggests that the satisfaction of men and women with sharing housework and childcare is heavily influenced by the quality of their marital relationship rather than by the actual distribution of household tasks[10].

The division of labour between men and women at home and in the work place sustains, and indeed is sustained by, the notion that mothers are the natural experts in the care of children. In fact there is a growing body of research to indicate that the parenting styles of mothers and fathers within couples is remarkably similar; where fathering differs from mothering, this is more strongly associated with situation than with gender[11]. As soon as fathers take similar levels of responsibility for young children as mothers, parenting approaches generally become indistinguishable[12].

The growing interest in the role of fathers within families is itself shaped by a number of factors including the diversification of family forms such as two parent families based on cohabitation and remarriage as well as one parent families constituted through divorce and births outside marriage, the effect of which is to create a typology of fathers – single fathers, non-resident fathers, step-fathers, etc. – having varying levels of involvement with their children and equally varying legal rights and social supports for that involvement. In addition, the relationship between families and work is changing such that, as we shall see in Chapter Two, fathers are no longer the sole providers in the majority of families which itself has created the expectation that since mothers and fathers share the providing role they should also share the childcare role.

Beyond these factors there is also a growing appreciation, supported by research, of the significance which fathers have in the lives of children as well as the value which involved fathering has for fathers as well as mothers. According to one leading commentator: "Fatherhood is, and always has been, about more than just the financial support of families. Fathers have an equally important role in the emotional, social and psychological development of their children and the support of their children's mother. This is more fundamental than sharing childcare and domestic work, increasingly important though this is, as breadwinning becomes more equitable. Being a father is also about helping young boys and girls develop conceptions of themselves in relation to men as well as women and encouraging them to understand and be comfortable with masculinity and maleness. It is about helping young people understand the dynamics of

"Within the last decade someone upped the ante on the tokens required for manhood. A generation ago providing for one's family was the only economic requirement. Nowadays, supplying the necessities entitles a man only to marginal respect. If your work allows you only to survive you are judged to be not much of a man. To be poor in a consumerist society is to have failed the manhood test".

SAM KEEN, 1991.

"Child-rearing needs to be acknowledged as a satisfying experience which can lead to personal growth (and which fathers are too often denied), rather than as a burden (which they are lucky to escape)"

ADRIENNE BURGESS AND SANDY RUXTON, 1996:IX.

8   See for example Marsiglio, 1995; Hawkins, Christiansen, Pond Sargent and Hill, 1995; O'Leary and Arias, 1988
9   Kiley, 1995:148
10 McKeown, Haase, Pratschke, Rock and Kidd, 2001; McKeown, Haase and Pratschke, 2001
11 Lewis, 1996
12 Gbrich, 1987

relationships in general and close relationships in particular. ... The consequences of fathers being absent from children's lives can ... be severe for children and parents alike"[13].

The importance of fathers to family life generally and to children in particular is clearly demonstrated by research as the summary of key findings in Table 1.2 shows.

Table 1.2 Key Research Findings on Fathers

- Fathers are the main carers for children while mothers are working.
- Most men say they enjoy having close relationships with their children. Indeed fathers from a diversity of social and ethnic backgrounds usually say that fathering is the most important part of their lives.
- A parent's gender is far less important in affecting child development than broader qualities such as warmth and kindness.
- Fathers who have participated in baby-care courses take on more care of their babies than fathers who have not.
- Men feel deeply moved by the experience of childbirth. Nine out of ten fathers attend the delivery of their babies.
- Mothers report that fathers are their main source of emotional support after the birth.
- Men who feel positive about their work are especially able to cope with the demands of a new baby.
- There is no difference between men's and women's patterns of arousal in response to their newborn babies.
- Fathers are as sensitive and responsive to their young children as mothers are.
- How fathers spend time with their young children is more important to the father-child relationship than how often they are with them.
- Fathers and mothers give their babies the same amount of affection.
- Babies usually "bond" as easily with their fathers as with their mothers.
- Some studies suggest that fathers help particularly in preparing the child for the outside world and developing "social skills".
- When fathers are involved with their children before the age of 11, they are more likely to escape having a criminal record by the age of 21.
- Non-resident fathers often have a strong presence in their children's lives. Most studies have shown that the children who fare best after divorce are those who see their fathers most often. However, a good father-child relationship usually reflects a harmonious relationship between the parents.
- Step fathers often become more involved in domestic life than biological fathers.
- In 10 per cent of families affected by divorce the father is the parent with whom the children live for most or all of the time.

Source: Lewis and Warren, 2001

---

[13] Roberts, in Foreword to Burghes, Clarke and Cronin, 1997:8. Ceridwen Roberts is the Director of the Family Policy Studies Centre in London.

These considerations have led to the writing of this report, itself part of a growing body of writing on the general theme of fatherhood[14]. In addition to promoting understanding and appreciation, the purpose of the report is also to stimulate action in areas where the positive involvement of fathers in the lives of their children is at risk or insufficiently supported. Such an agenda for action is not just for fathers; it is also for children and their mothers and for the promotion of family well-being in whatever form the family takes[15]

A key theme which informs the report is that no one should be left out of the family picture. An inclusive society requires an inclusive family. Mothers, fathers and children, including the extended family, are all part of the family picture which, for all the vicissitudes of family life, is part of the reality to which everyone belongs; family histories are dotted by the abiding presences of absent members. At various times in history, ways of thinking about the family have tended to displace, distort or simply ignore the lived experiences of different family members be they mothers, children or fathers and, inevitably, new ways of thinking about families have always emerged to redirect attention towards these blind spots. This report is part of a process of keeping fathers in the family picture alongside mothers and children and, as such, is based on the belief that an inclusive family helps to create an inclusive society.

[14] In addition to the growing corpus of reports, books and articles on fathers, there is also a plethora of valuable websites on the topic which can be accessed using "father" as the search word. One report has estimated that 700 research papers have been produced annually over the past 20 years on the theme of fathers (Lewis and Warin, 2001:1).
[15] See McKeown and Sweeney, 2001

Is the Role of Fathers Changing?

"Marriage and parenthood are becoming increasingly separate institutions."

<small>JUDITH SELTZER AND YVONNE BRNADRETH, 1994:51</small>

The role of father, in its most basic form, involves a relationship with a child that embraces the biological and the psychological as well as the social and economic. Fatherhood, like motherhood, is also a social construct which, in Western society, has traditionally been built around marriage. The marriage contract has traditionally involved a division of labour between fathers and mothers such that fathers worked as breadwinners outside the home while mothers worked as carers inside the home. This arrangement, whose ideal is embodied in the Irish Constitution, meant that "good fathers" were essentially "good providers" and their role was more about "financial investment" than "emotional involvement"; conversely, "good mothers" were seen as women who stayed at home to look after the children. In order to understand how the role of fathers is changing it is necessary to look at how the traditional model of family in Ireland is also changing.

A brief snapshot of families in Ireland is presented in Table 2.1. This describes families in terms of the number of parents living in the same household and the number of earners working in that household. From this it emerges that the traditional model of family is still the norm for around half of all Irish families, that is, families where two parents live together and the father is the sole breadwinner. However, as Table 2.1 also shows, families now take more diverse forms.

In Ireland, the vast majority of parents (86%) live with each other although a significant minority (14%) live in one parent households[16]. Between 1986 and 1996, one parent households where at least one child is under the age of 15, increased by 89% while the corresponding number of two parent households decreased by 9% in the same period; similarly and within the same period, the proportion of children living in one parent households grew by 50% while the proportion living in two parent households declined by 21%[17]. These are indicative of dramatic changes in household composition and family relationships and effectively result in a growing proportion of non-resident fathers; at the same time, it is worth emphasising that the vast majority of households (86%) and children (88%) have two resident parents.

More than anything else, work has become the main factor impacting on families and the parenting roles of men and women. The world of work is changing the role of fathers in two important ways. The first is through the growing involvement of mothers in the labour force whose effect is to increase the number of two earner families, thereby altering the role of fathers as the sole breadwinner in those families. In 1996, as revealed in Table 2.1, nearly four out of ten households had two earners; this proportion has almost certainly increased since then as the labour force participation rate of women increased from 39% in 1996 to 47% in 2000, close the EU average while the corresponding participation rates for men, at around the EU average of 70%, remained virtually unchanged[18]. Fathers, in other words, are

---

[16] A range of terminology has evolved to describe the reality of families where both parents do not live together, notably "one parent households", "non-resident parents" and "one parent families". This terminology reflects an assumption that families and households are the same thing. This assumption is accurate in many cases but the growth of marital breakdown, births outside marriage and the reconstitution of families through re-marriage or cohabitation, makes it much less accurate as a description of the diversity found among modern families. Indeed the tendency to conflate households with families has the effect, however unintended, of excluding large numbers of non-resident parents (mostly fathers) and fails to acknowledge the reality that a person – both adult and child – is still a member of a family even if not living in the same household. These reflections on the difference between a family and a household are far from pedantic since they have a deep influence on how we conceptualise the family, how membership of families is defined and measured and what policy measures are adopted to promote the well-being of family members.

no longer the sole providers in an increasing proportion of two parent households.

The situation in one parent households is dramatically different with a majority (64%) having no earner in 1996; this however is also likely to have changed since then as more lone mothers have entered employment; indeed lone mothers are now more likely than any other category of mother to be in the labour force[19]. Nevertheless the employment patterns in one and two parent households draws attention to the emergence of a polarisation between "work rich" and "work poor" families which has been observed in other EU countries. In Britain, for example, it has been found that the proportion of dual-earner and no-earner families has grown at the expense of one-earner families[20]. No comparable data on this trend exists in Ireland. It has also been found that dual-earner families in Britain, as in Ireland, tend to be better qualified and to have higher status and higher paid jobs while those with no earner tended to be the opposite[21].

The second, and possibly more important, factor affecting the role of fathers is the amount of hours they work outside the home. On average, Irish fathers work 46 hours per week although a third of fathers work 50 hours per week or more even if, under The Organisation of Working Time Act, 1997, the maximum working week is 48 hours[22]. Mothers typically work an average of 15 hours per week less than fathers. Fathers are also more likely to work unsocial hours than mothers: two thirds of fathers do Saturday work, nearly half do evening work, and two fifths do Sunday work, and a quarter do night work. In general, Irish fathers and mothers seem to work longer hours outside the home than most of their EU counterparts, with the possible exception of Britain.

"The differences between the sexes is being eroded as both sexes become defined by work. It is often said that the public world of work is a man's place and that as women enter it they will become increasingly 'masculine' and lose their 'femininity'. To think this way is to miss the most important factor of the economic world. Economic man, the creature who defines itself within the horizons of work and consumption, is not man in any full sense of the word, but a being who has been neutralised, degendered, rendered subservient to the laws of the market. The danger of economics is not that it turns women into men but that it destroys the fullness of both manhood and womanhood."

SAM KEEN, 1991:65.

Table 2.1 Number of Income Earners in One and Two Parent Households, 1996

Category	Two Parent Household %	One Parent Household %
No Earner	11	64
One Earner	50	36
Two Earner	39	0
Total (Column %)*	100	100
Total (Row %)**	86	14

In this table the concept of family is restricted to those families where there is at least one child under the age of 15.
*   Based on special tabulations of the Labour Force Survey, 1996.
**   Based on the Census of Population, 1996.

"Unlike women, men who have children are not routinely distinguished in official statistics from those who do not."

LOUIE BURGHES, LYNDA CLARKE AND NATALIE CRONIN, 1997:87

---

[17] See McKeown and Sweeney, 2001, Chapter Two.
[18] See Labour Force Survey, 1996; Quarterly National Household Survey, 2000; see also Nolan, O'Connell and Whelan, 2000.
[19] McKeown and Sweeney, 2001, Chapter Two.
[20] Burghes, Clarke, and Cronin, 1997, Chapter Four.
[21] Ferri and Smith, 1996

"There is no sign that fathers are reducing their working hours in response to the increased employment and working hours of mothers."

JULIA BRANNEN, PETER MOSS, CHARLIE OWEN AND CHRIS WALE, 1997:129

"True reconciliation between work and family requires fathers' needs to be addressed alongside mothers."

ADRIENNE BURGESS AND SANDY RUXTON, 1996:X

The growth in employment by mothers combined with the continuing long hours worked by fathers means that the total volume of hours worked outside the home by the parents of dependent children continues to rise, particularly among higher socio-economic groups. This adds to the polarisation of "work rich" and "work poor" families and has major implications for household income, the management of household work and caring and the welfare of family members, especially children, with different challenges facing families who are income poor compared to those who are time poor[23].

The powerful influence exercised by work in drawing parents out of the home stands in stark contrast to the growing expectations in society generally that parents – but especially fathers – should be spending more time with their children. Parenting can be seen as having two interrelated dimensions: the provider or "investment" role and the caring or "involvement" role. Traditionally, the father's role was around investment while the mother's role was around involvement. Increasingly however there is an expectation, shared by fathers as well as mothers, that fathers should provide increasing amounts of both investment and involvement. Attitude surveys still show that both men and women see "investment" as central to the father role[24] while also showing that fathers should have more "involvement" in the upbringing of their children[25].

These developments place fathers in an awkward psychological position because investment without involvement no longer caries the esteem that it once did. Ironically, the father's investment role may be esteemed by the mother but not the children and its effect, however unintentional, may be to strengthen the mother's relationship with the children while weakening the father's. Many fathers are experiencing the stress of having to combine both investment with involvement roles and, being unable to rely on the role model of their own father, are having to learn new ways of being a father. Of course, many mothers are experiencing similar stress.

There is a growing recognition in policy circles that many parents have difficulty reconciling the competing demands of work and family to the satisfaction of their employers, their children and their partners. In recognition of this, a number of EU countries have introduced - or are introducing - measures designed to make the workplace more family-friendly and flexible so that parents can become more involved in the care of their children while at the same time being more available for work. Family-friendly initiatives cover a wide range of measures including flexible working (job-sharing, flexitime, working from home, part-time working, etc.), leave arrangements (maternity leave, paternity leave, adoption leave, etc.), breaks (employment breaks, sabbaticals, secondments, etc.), and other initiatives (such as childcare support, employee assistance programmes, etc)[26].

---

[22] Based on special tabulations of the 1996 Labour Force Survey.
[23] See Brannen, Moss, Owen and Wale, 1997:135-136
[24] See, for example, the evidence cited in Lewis, 2000:6.
[25] Eurobarometer, 1993; Whelan and Fahey, 1994.

During the 1990s, a raft of reports created a consensus between the Irish Government and the social partners on the need to develop family friendly measures in employment, particularly in the area of childcare; these reports include national plans[27], national agreements[28] and expert reports[29]. In different ways, the measures proposed have the potential to facilitate greater involvement by fathers in the care of their children and families although they cannot entirely obviate the need for each family to make difficult decisions on how to allocate time between work and family life, career and children.

One of the features of family friendly measures is that fathers - and men generally - are less likely to avail of them than women and mothers. This was amply confirmed in a study of flexible working in Ireland which showed that "job sharing, career breaks and extended parental leave encourage more women than men to trade full-time continuous jobs and careers for extra time off"[30]. As a result, family-friendly measures can leave men's working lives almost untouched and can reinforce existing gender differences between men and women both at work and at home, as fathers work full-time and mothers work part-time[31].

The reasons why men and fathers are slow to take up flexible working arrangements, even when they are available[32], are similar in Ireland as elsewhere; they include loss of earnings which can have a negative effect on the entire family, increased workload resulting from taking time off and the fear that taking leave for family reasons may have a negative impact on one's career, itself a reflection of how men's self-identity is often turned and sometimes torn more towards work than family. In addition, the culture of the workplace can discourage men from availing of family friendly measures because it does not expect men who are fathers to behave any differently to men who are not fathers.

In addition, the response of men and fathers to flexible working arrangements may itself be influenced by the way in which those measures are presented and promoted. In Ireland, most of the arguments in favour of family-friendly measures in the workplace are advanced from the perspective of women's equality in the labour market. The same also appears to be the case in other countries and this may help to explain why women rather than men make most use of these measures[33]. It also needs to be emphasised that family friendly measures, as the term is normally used, do not cover the number of hours worked by fathers even though this is one of the more important factors determining employed fathers' involvement with children. In essence, family-friendly measures will only be effective in improving the balance between work and family life - and promoting joint parenting - if their net effect is to create real choices for couples, including reducing the excessive hours worked by some fathers. Even more pointedly, it also needs to be recognised that balancing work and family life is more than a matter

"Policies must support men and women so that they can create whatever kind of family arrangements satisfy both partners' images of life as a family"

C.P. COWAN AND P.A. COWAN, 1988A:171.

"Family-friendly policy making for men is not the same as family-friendly policy making for women."

ADRIENNE BURGESS, 1997:163.

[26] See Humphreys, Fleming and O'Donnell, 2000.
[27] Government of Ireland, 1993; 1999.
[28] Government of Ireland, 1996; 2000.
[29] Second Commission on the Status of Women, 1993; Employment Equality Agency, 1996; McKeown, 1997; Commission on the Family, 1998; National Economic and Social Council, 1996; 1999; Partnership 2000 Expert Working Group on Childcare, 1999.
[30] Fynes, Morrissey, Roche, Whelan and Williams, 1996.
[31] It is significant that three quarters of all part-time work in Ireland in 2000 was undertaken by women although this should be seen in the context that only 17% of all employment is part-time so that, in general, women, like men, are much more likely to be in full-time than part-time employment (Quarterly National Household Survey, 2000).
[32] See, for example, a review of the Danish experience in Schultz Jorgensen, 1991 which shows that while large numbers of fathers take paternity leave very few seem to use other types of leave available to them.

11

of public policy; it is also a matter within their own family and the adjustments in roles and expectations, resources and routines which this will inevitably entail.

The changes which are now taking place in Irish families, many of them induced by the greater involvement of parents in the world of work and the corresponding rise in expectations about the need to spend more time at home with the family have created more choices and challenges for both fathers and mothers. How parents respond to these choices and challenges is strongly influenced by their social class position but also, and particularly in the case of fathers, by whether they are married and living with their children. Becoming a father, it seems, is not as simple as it used to be!

---

[33] See for example Carlsen, 1993.

It is hard to state precisely where the process of becoming a father begins: at the moment of the child's conception? at the birth of the child? or when the baby is first planned? The vagueness of the father's relationship to the child - and of his rights to the child while in the womb - mirrors the vagueness of the father's role in general and is probably independent of the father's marital or residential status. It is only in relatively recent times that fathers wanted to be present at the birth of their children.

It is true that registering of the birth of a child is of enormous legal significance for both parents but this is a purely bureaucratic procedure without any ritual or ceremony to match its initiatory importance for parents. Moreover only married fathers have an automatic entitlement to be registered as fathers of their child. Of course baptism is a public religious ritual which welcomes the child into society and, by virtue of that, is a public expression of how men and women are initiated into motherhood and fatherhood respectively. The statistics suggest that baptism still remains a popular ritual[34].

By comparison with the process of becoming a mother - which is clearly signalled in the woman's pregnancy and the physical changes in her body over nine months before giving birth - the process of becoming a father normally has no outward signs for a man. "Women do have the biological edge with infants", according to some psychologists[35]. "They have wombs, they create the milk, they have a great abundance of attachment hormones rushing through their bodies after birth"[36]. A woman's motherhood is never in doubt once she has given birth whereas a man's fatherhood is always a matter of presumption. The psychological consequences of this are explained by one Jungian analyst as follows: "The male's lack of any physical experience, beyond copulation, in the bearing and delivering of the child, leaves his psychic relationship at a primitive, almost magical level. Fatherhood seems to be more about the acceptance of paternity than the impregnation of the female. The father's acceptance of paternity demonstrates the emergence of the generations within history"[37].

Pregnancy therefore is the period when women prepare and - through ante-natal visits and classes as well as reading books and leaflets - are prepared for motherhood. Moreover, while men cannot get pregnant, it has been assumed, at least until recently, that men do not need to be involved in the ante-natal process of preparing for fatherhood. Even books on pregnancy, childbirth and child rearing tend to be directed at women rather than men[38]. Indeed, as one researcher has pointed out: "Structural disincentives for male involvement in pregnancy are legion. .... Antenatal classes are given by women, are overwhelmingly directed at women and, to accommodate hospital and tutors' schedules, are generally held during the day, with, at the most, one 'father's evening' and one hospital tour scheduled. Antenatal

How Are Men Initiated Into Fatherhood?

"Until quite recently, the father's role in raising the children was simply ignored."

ARTHUR COLMAN AND LIBBY COLMAN, 1988:185.

---

[34] In 1997 there were 66,096 Catholic baptisms in Ireland, north and south (see Annuarium Statisticum Ecclesiae, 1987 and 1997). If Catholic births were strictly proportional to the size of the Catholic population in the Republic of Ireland (92%) and in Northern Ireland (42%), this would yield 58,669 births which is less than the actual number of Catholic baptisms (66,096) in that year! Clearly the explanation for this must lie in the fact that Catholics, especially in the north but also in the south, have a higher fertility rate than other groups (Coleman, 1999); also, it seems likely from these figures that most Catholic children are baptised.
[35] Colman and Colman, 1988:xvii
[36] ibid
[37] Ryce-Menuhin, 1996:74

13

"Men feel deeply moved by the experience of childbirth. Nine out of ten fathers attend the delivery of their babies these days. Not only is this a miraculous event, it also is remembered by many dads as a time when they feel an intense commitment which · · becomes lasting."

CHARLIE LEWIS AND JO WARIN, 2001:3.

"Women's work is frequently invisible as is men's parenting."

JO WARIN, YVETTE SOLOMON, CHARLIE LEWIS AND WENDY LANGFORD, 1999:42.

appointments are also held in the daytime, and there is no awareness among professionals of any need to improve upon a casual invitation to fathers. .... The average expectant father is killed off through lack of interest, his concern tolerated at best … by health professionals completely out of touch with paternal experience"[39]. A similar view has been expressed by a Swedish gynaecologist after he became a father: "I became a father for the first time in 1978 when I was 36. In my case it became a decisive event in my life, and that includes my professional life. By then, I had acquired considerable experience as a specialist in gynaecology and childbirth. … . It struck me that in my encounters with all those couples, I had spontaneously turned to the women, since they were clearly the most 'important' persons. I had only occasionally focused directly on the men, and this also applied to emotional questions, fear, expectations and anxiety or happiness prior to birth and parenthood. And yet I am a man myself. Why wasn't it natural for me to also be able to 'see' men on their own terms? Eventually, I began to understand that there were several aspects to these difficulties and inner obstacles. As a man - despite my profession - I did not have the words or language for men's feelings and experiences in connection with childbirth and fatherhood"[40].

The process of becoming a father therefore, both before and after the child's birth, is heavily laced with signals to indicate that the primary parent is the mother and the secondary parent is the father; many mothers and fathers subscribe to, and reinforce, this division of labour irrespective of their marital status. The father's main role is seen to support the mother whose views on how to look after the child are treated as paramount. Even the existence of maternity but not paternity leave from work reinforces the social image of the mother as the primary carer of the child; it is recognised, of course, that maternity leave is also important to allow the mother time to recover physically from the birth of the child. These observations simply indicate that the journey to parenthood is quite different for mothers and fathers and often the process does little or nothing to prepare fathers for involvement with the child.

These considerations suggest that some of the existing conventions surrounding pregnancy, childbirth and child rearing may need re-examination if men are to identify more fully with the fatherhood role. It might be asked, for example, if ante-natal classes are sufficiently inclusive of and sympathetic to men? Does the information provided through text, pictures, and videos portray a full and positive role for fathers? Is it appropriate that there is no paternity leave for fathers which would facilitate bonding with their new-born child just as there is maternity leave for mothers in recognition of the physical demands of childbearing and breast-feeding? Much of the research evidence suggests that, with better preparation for fatherhood and parenthood, the attachment between father and child - as well as between father and mother - can be greatly strengthened; in addition, fathers become more involved with the child after its birth[41].

---

[38] An exception to this trend is the excellently written book, Becoming a Father: How to Make a Success of Your Role as a Parent by Mike Lilley (1997). Fathers Direct, a UK organisation, have brought out the Bounty Guide to Fatherhood which is also excellent.

[39] Burgess, 1997:112-113

[40] Swedin, 1995.

[41] Jackson, 1984; Nickel and Kocher, 1987; Cowan and Cowan, 1988b; Brazelton and Cramer, 1991

The well-being of children is influenced by many factors both inside and outside the family. Within the family, research[42] consistently points out that the well-being of children, as measured according to a variety of indicators, is influenced by two key factors: (1) the family's economic or material well-being and (2) the family's relational well-being which covers both parent-parent relationships and parent-child relationships. Fathers, like mothers, have a crucial influence on both these aspects of well-being and it is through these channels that one is most likely to find the influence of fathers on the well-being of children.

Before examining the research evidence it might be useful to consider the opening lines of Frank McCourt's book Angela's Ashes: Memoir of Childhood which won the 1997 US Pulitzer Prize: "When I look back on my childhood I wonder how I survived at all. It was, of course, a miserable childhood: the happy childhood is hardly worth your while. Worse than the ordinary miserable childhood is the miserable Irish childhood, and worse yet is the miserable Irish Catholic childhood. People everywhere brag and whimper about the woes of early childhood, but nothing can compare with the Irish version: the poverty; the shiftless loquacious alcoholic father; the pious defeated mother moaning by the fire; the pompous priests; bullying schoolmasters; the English and the terrible things they did to us for eight hundred long years".

What does this example teach us? One of the things it teaches is that no one is simply the product of his or her parents. Every person is much more than their conditioning; there is nature as well as nurture in each. Parents get blamed for many things but it is a fallacy - a "parental fallacy", according to one psychologist[43] - to think that we are only what our parents make us. Indeed the influence which parents exercise on their children may be more complicated and less obvious than is commonly believed, as Carl Jung (1875-1961) has argued: "children are driven unconsciously in a direction that is intended to compensate for everything that was left unfulfilled in the lives of their parents"[44]. This is worth remembering when reading about the influence of parents on children.

A first key finding to emerge from research is that the well-being of children as measured in terms of educational outcomes (such as completion of second and third level education) is heavily influenced by the income level of parents, particularly the income of parents when the child is under the age of five[45]. Given that households from which the father is absent – which make up the vast majority of one parent households – tend to be poorer than two parent households, it is tempting to conclude that the absence of fathers has a negative effect on the educational outcomes of children because their absence makes those households poorer. This conclusion is true, but only partly. The part that is true, at least as regards research in Ireland, is that one parent households have a consistently higher risk of poverty than those two parent households in which both parents are working. The part that is not

What Impact Do Fathers Have on Children?

"Our lives may be determined less by our childhood than by the way we have learned to imagine our childhoods. We are ... less damaged by the traumas of childhood than by the traumatic way we remember childhood"

JAMES HILLMAN, 1996.

---

[42] See, for example, Amato, 1993; Amato and Keith, 1991; Amato, Loomis and Booth, 1995; Cooksey, 1997; Downey, 1994; Goodman, Emery and Haugaard, 1998; Hetherington and Stanley-Hagan, 1997; Hines, 1997; McLanahan, 1997; McLanahan and Sandefur, 1994; McLanahan and Teitler, 1999; Najman, Behrens, Andersen, Bor, O'Callaghan, and Williams, 1997; Seltzer, 1994; Thomson, Hanson and McLanahan, 1994

[43] According to James Hillman, "If any fantasy holds our contemporary civilisation in an unyielding grip, it is that we are our parents' children and that the primary instrument of our fate is the behavior of your mother and father" (Hillman, 1996:63).

[44] Jung, 1925:191

[45] Duncan & Brooks-Gunn, 1997; see also Cameron, & Heckman, 1999; McLanahan, 1997.

"Nothing has a more powerful influence upon children than the life their parents have not lived."

CARL JUNG, 1994

true is when one parent households are compared to two parent household in which there is only one earner; in this comparison, both sets of households have broadly similar risks of poverty. The reason for this is because, when these households are compared and account is taken of both the socio-economic status of the parents[46]and the number of children[47], the risk of poverty is almost the same. Indeed it is precisely because lone parents tend to be in a weaker socio-economic position than other parents[48] that the proportion of one parent households living in poverty (29%) tends to be higher than the corresponding proportion of two parent households (19%)[49].

This point is worth making in order to indicate that the cause of poverty in one parent households is often due to the socio-economic characteristics of those households rather than the absence of fathers – although the absence of fathers may itself be due to their weak socio-economic and employment status. This is certainly consistent with the fact that a man's marriage and parenting prospects are strongly influenced by his economic prospects: men with poor economic prospects also have poorer marriage prospects[50] while men who are non-resident fathers are more likely to lose contact with their children if they are poor[51].

It is also worth pointing out that, as dual earning becomes the norm in two parent families, the relative position of all one earner and no earner families is bound to deteriorate. In these circumstances, the relative risk of poverty in one parent families is likely to continue to rise. This means that the economic viability of households without fathers is likely to deteriorate as dual earning become the norm and this, in turn, could have a deleterious effect on the educational well-being of children. This analysis does not allow us to claim that the absence of fathers from households causes a deterioration in educational outcomes of children although it does allow us to affirm that, other things being equal, the presence of fathers improves the material well-

[46] For example, a two parent household where there are two children with the father working and the mother on home duties has a broadly similar risk of poverty (11.3%) to a lone parent household where the mother has one child, belongs to social class 5 and is working (13.4%) (See Nolan and Watson: 1999: Tables 3.2 and 3.5, pp.46–55). By contrast, the risk of poverty in a lone mother household where the mother has one child, belongs to social class 5 and is working is extremely high (80%) and is surpassed only by risk of poverty experienced by lone fathers (87%) in similar circumstances (see Nolan and Watson, 1999: Table 3.2, p.46). As Watson and Nolan observe, "when one controls for other factors, female-headed households have a lower risk of poverty than non-couple households headed by males" (ibid:47).

[47] For example, the risk of poverty to children rises with the number of children so that two parent households with four or more children have a similar risk of poverty (45.4%) to children in one parent households (44.4%) (see Nolan, 2000: Table 4.6, p.45).

[48] See McKeown, 2001, Table 3, p.9.

[49] Nolan and Watson, 1999, Table 2.1, p.18. Of course we know nothing about the risk of poverty among non-resident fathers

[50] In Ireland in 1991, for example, the proportion of single men aged 45–54 in the unskilled manual category was 2.5 times higher than the corresponding proportion of single men in the lower professional category; moreover this association between marriage prospects and economic prospects can be traced over many decades. A few years ago, a team of researchers at the ESRI made a similar point: "The Irish State's policies combine today to perpetuate and even exacerbate class inequalities in family formation and functioning. The life chance of marriage is now more strongly related to one's class of origin as are fertility differentials" (Breen, Hannan, Rottman and Whelan, 1990:121). Similarly in the US, low male earnings not only reduce the likelihood of marriage but also increase the likelihood of divorce (Levine and Pitt, 1995:37) while it has also been argued that the "inability to provide is the root cause of father absence for African American children (Morehouse Research Institute, 1999:12; Wilson, 1996). There is also research evidence which suggests that some women may prefer the prospect of lone parenthood than share child rearing with a young unemployed father (Wilson and Neckerman, 1986; Roberts, 1996). Faced with these circumstances, it is inevitable that young men in disadvantaged communities may face the double exclusion from the worlds of work and family life and are "an extremely excluded and ostracised group in Ireland today" (McKeown, 2001).

[51] In a survey of 619 non-resident fathers in the UK in 1995, the authors found that "contact is much more regular if the father is in employment" (Bradshaw, Stimson, Skinner and Williams, 1999a:98).

being of households which, in turn, is strongly associated with beneficial educational outcomes for those children. In that sense, it is true to say that fathers are beneficial to the material and educational well-being of children, a conclusion which is consistent with other studies which suggest that "the contribution of resources, both economic and psychological, from fathers may be the key contributing factor in the educational achievement of young adults"[52].

These considerations indicate how important the providing role is within families – whether performed by fathers, mothers or both – while also highlighting the complementary role of the State in promoting the well-being of families through income transfers and family support services. As we have already seen, children's educational achievements in particular are known to be heavily influenced by the material well-being of their families.

A second key finding to emerge from research is that the well-being of children as measured in terms of the absence of psychological problems (such as behaviour or emotional difficulties) is heavily influenced by the relational well-being of their family. In particular, children are adversely affected by conflict and instability within the family. Indeed it is precisely because conflict and instability are usually key processes leading to the formation of one parent households that children in these households tend to do less well in behavioural and psychological terms than children in two parent households. That is a clear finding from a meta-analysis of 12 different US studies which found that "family structure is more important than poverty in determining behavioural and psychological problems"[53]. Numerous other studies have come up with the same result[54], including some Irish studies[55]

In addition it has also been established that instability, even in the absence of conflict, has detrimental effects on children has also been replicated elsewhere. One US longitudinal study covering 20 years which interviewed children when they reached the age of 19 found that "for offspring from low conflict homes, parental divorce was devastating" in terms of psychological distress, support networks and marital happiness[56]. Moreover, 70% of the divorces in this study involved minor rather than severe marital conflict and this indicates the powerful inter-generational impact of instability on the well-being of children. The author observed: "The most discouraging thing about these findings is the evidence of inter-generational effects. The marriages of children of divorce whose parents did not fight are of lower quality than they would be if their parents had not dissolved their marriage. Not only does this mean that the children of such parents are more likely to divorce themselves, but that their children are apt to experience the same adverse consequences of divorce as their parents. Unless the divorce rate declines, we can expect the same high levels of personal disorganisation in generations to come"[57].

"A child's experience of a loving relationship between its parents – and not just with its parents - may contribute more to its well-being than additional income or having a bedroom of its own".

MCKEOWN AND SWEENEY, 2001:52

[52] Furstenberg, 1990:155.
[53] McLanahan, 1997.
[54] Amato, 1993; Amato and Keith, 1991; Amato, Loomis and Booth, 1995; Cooksey, 1997; Downey, 1994; Goodman, Emery and Haugaard, 1998; Hetherington and Stanley-Hagan, 1997; Hines, 1997; McLanahan and Sandefur, 1994; McLanahan and Teitler, 1999; Najman, Behrens, Andersen, Bor, O'Callaghan, and Williams, 1997; Seltzer, 1994; Thomson, Hanson and McLanahan, 1994
[55] Flanagan, 2001; O'Donohoe, 2001
[56] Booth, 1999:40
[57] ibid:41

17

"It's never too late to have a happy childhood"

ANONYMOUS.

These results, representing the distilled consensus of different studies in different countries, show just how difficult it is to try to separate the influence of fathers from the rest of the family system. At the same time, they clearly show that fathers are important to the well-being of children. For example, the adverse consequences of separation and divorce on children, particularly in low conflict situations, cannot be unrelated to the absence of fathers in the lives of those children. Similarly the benign effects of stable two parent families must also reflect the benign effects which fathers, no less than mothers, have on the well-being of children. One review summarised the implications of this research as follows: "In sum, research suggests that if we are concerned about optimising children's health and development, we should be promoting and supporting both two-parent family structure plus ways to involve fathers in their children's lives – whatever the family form"[58].

A particularly interesting feature of the studies we have reviewed is the way in which parent-parent relationships emerge as central to the well-being of children[59] essentially because this relationship, according to one leading team of US researchers, "is bound up with virtually every dimension of offspring well-being"[60]. This view is echoed by another researcher who suggests that involved fathering promotes positive child development in the following way: "the benefits obtained by children with highly involved fathers are largely attributable to the fact that high levels of paternal involvement created family contexts in which parents felt good about their marriages and the child care arrangements they had been able to work out"[61]. This suggests that services to promote the well-being of children need to focus not just on material well-being but also on relational well-being through parent-child as well as parent-parent relationships.

The research reviewed so far in this chapter is mainly in the "behaviourist" or "empiricist" tradition and focused on the measurable outcomes for children in those family circumstances which allowed us to draw some conclusions about the impact of fathers. However there is an older tradition within psychology, beginning with Sigmund Freud (1856-1939) and continuing through psychoanalysis and attachment theory, which has also reflected on the dynamics of the family system as constituted by the relationships between mother, father and child. Freud saw the mother's relationship with the child as fundamental to the child's survival because it allows the child to internalise a model of safety and trust which is the basis for healthy development and for future relationships. Despite the importance and intensity of the mother-child relationship, it needs to enter a process of separation in order to avoid its potentially destructive closeness. For the child, separation allows new identifications and new possibilities in the world. For the mother, separation gives back her sense of self, separateness and independence.

The father is the key player in this process of separation, acting as the 'other', or the third person, to the mother. Within the present structure of the nuclear family in the Western world, the father is normally the biological

---

[58] Levine and Pitt, 1995, p.25.
[59] The impact of parent-parent relationships on child well-being is considerably more pronounced in conventional two parent families compared to stepfamilies as one review of the research suggests: "The differences between intact and stepfamilies suggest that stepfamilies do not necessarily function in the same ways as first-marriage families. The parents' partnership does not have such a direct influence on the parent-child and sibling relationships, and stepchildren have a comparatively strong influence on parental behaviour, especially in the early years" (Harold, Pryor and Reynolds, 2001:5).
[60] Amato and Booth, 1997:221
[61] Lamb, 1997.

father; however it is possible that the "father figure" is neither a father nor even a man. What is essential from the psychoanalytic perspective is that the father figure must be someone other than the mother who moves the two person mother-child relationship into a three person "triangular" relationship of mother-child-father. In psychoanalysis, the father is seen as fundamental to the child letting go of the mother because: (1) he symbolically prohibits the potentially incestuous closeness and attachment of the child to the mother and (2) he symbolically promises and represents new and more exciting ways of being in the world. The father is also fundamental to the mother in letting go of the child: he is the person who sustains part of the mother's desire and meets this desire. Psychoanalysis teaches that unless the father takes up his position representing the symbolic order for the child and the mother, the separation process can become frustrated resulting in various neuroses and disturbances for the child and indeed for the relationship, the family and society.

The psychoanalytic perspective, particularly as articulated by Jacques Lacan (1901-1981)and others, restores fathers - and the father figure - to a central place within family life, on a par with mothers. The reason why the father is given such a prominent role in the psychoanalytic perspective is simply due to the fact that the nuclear family of mother-child-father is central to the organisation of society in the western world. It is crucial that the child experiences, at the deepest level of its being, an awareness of these structures and is initiated into the world through the key figures of mother and father. That is why fatherhood is not just practically important; it is symbolically important as well.

These psychological insights offer another perspective on how the well-being of children is influenced by relationships with their parents as well as by the relationships which parents have with each other. The broader implication of this chapter for family policy and family practice is that family well-being has a dual aspect – both material and relational – which needs to be supported and promoted. Adopting such an approach is known to the in the best interests of children and their parents[62]. In addition, this approach to family policy and practice will help to ensure that the specific needs of fathers are not overlooked by service providers as sometimes happens, a theme to which we return in Chapter Eight below.

"It is overwhelmingly to the social order, as it is concretised in the family, and to the place that social order allows the father to assume, almost independently of his personal qualities, that Freud and Lacan direct our attention. In our contemporary production-oriented world everything has conspired to diminish the place of the Father, and the process has been powerfully assisted by a psychology too preoccupied with the gratification and frustration of need to realise that this perspective overlooks an essential dimension of human reality."

CORMAC GALLAGHER, 1986:138.

---

[62] See McKeown and Sweeney, 2001.

How Does the Law Treat Fathers?

"The law still focuses on the relationship between mother and father, rather than the father and the child. We need fundamental reform of this legislation which will give legal recognition to the importance of fatherhood".

SUZANNE SPEAK, STUART CAMERON AND ROSE GILROY, 1997:34.

The family which is recognised and protected in the Irish Constitution (Articles 41 and 42) is based on marriage. By implication, the rights and responsibilities of fathers come through marriage; unmarried or "natural" fathers do not exist in the Constitution[63].

The Constitution makes no explicit reference to fathers, married or otherwise. Mothers are explicitly mentioned - if not to the delight of all women - in the context of their contribution to the common good by working at home (Article 41.2.1) and the need to ensure that they do not neglect their home duties by having to engage in outside work (Article 41.2.2)[64]. This might be seen as symptomatic of giving a greater social value to the ideology of motherhood and of symbolically strengthening motherhood over fatherhood.

In 1966, the Supreme Court clarified the following aspects of the Irish Constitution: (i) a natural or biological father is not a member of a family within Article 41; (ii) a natural or biological father is not a parent within Article 42; and (iii) a natural or biological father has no personal right in relation to his child which the State is bound to protect under Article 40.3 (The State (Nicolaou) v an Bord Uchtála).

In 1996, the Constitution Review Group acknowledged that "there has been much criticism of the continued constitutional ostracism of natural fathers" and proposed the following solution: "The Review Group considers that the solution [to giving constitutional rights to natural fathers] appears to lie in following the approach of Article 8 of the ECHR [European Convention on Human Rights] in guaranteeing to every person respect for 'family life' which has been interpreted to include non-marital family life but yet requiring the existence of family ties between the mother and the father. This may be a way of granting constitutional rights to those fathers who have, or had, a stable relationship with the mother prior to birth, or subsequent to birth with the child, while excluding persons from having such rights who are only biological fathers without any such relationship. In the context of the Irish constitution it would have to be made clear that the reference to family life included family life not based on marriage"[65].

The reference to Article 8 of the European Convention on Human Rights - involving the right to respect for family life - is significant in the Irish context since this was the basis of a successful legal action taken by an Irish unmarried father to the European Commission of Human Rights in 1991. The case was taken by Joseph Keegan who complained that his right to respect to family life had been violated because his child had been placed for adoption by its mother without his knowledge or consent; in addition, he complained that Irish law did not afford him even a defeasible right to be appointed guardian.

The facts of the case are that Joseph Keegan had a stable relationship with the mother of his child over a period of two years, during one of which they cohabited. The conception of their child was a deliberate decision by both of them and they had also planned to get married. In order to establish that Keegan's "right to respect for his family life" had been violated - which the European Court of Human Rights established - the Court first established that he had a family life in the following way: "The Court recalled that the

---

[63] I gratefully acknowledge the insightful comments on an earlier draft of this chapter from Margaret Dromey of Treoir: Federation of Services for Unmarried Parents and their Children.
[64] For interesting commentaries on how family and gender are constructed in the Irish Constitution, see, Martin, 1998; Dooley, 1998; Flynn, 1998
[65] Constitution Review Group, 1996:326.

notion of the "family" in this provision is not confined solely to marriage-based relationships and may encompass other de facto "family" ties where the parties are living together outside marriage. A child born out of such a relationship is ipso iure part of that "family" unit from the moment of his birth and by the very fact of it. There thus exists between the child and his parents a bond amounting to family life even if at the time of his or her birth the parents are no longer cohabiting or if their relationship has then ended"[66].

This judgement is significant in showing that one of the rocks upon which family and fatherhood rests is the social relations between the parents rather than solely on the physical or biological relationship to the child. A stable relationship between the parents - either before or since the birth of the child, or both - is thus seen as a minimal prerequisite to becoming a father. By the same token, the definition excludes those exceptional cases - such as rape or incest - where a normal relationship between the parents does not exist and any claims to fatherhood based on such a relationship would not be regarded as socially acceptable. However the definition fails to clarify those more nebulous cases where the parents did not have a steady relationship before or since the birth of the child but each may wish to develop a bond with their child.

The existing situation in Ireland regarding the rights of unmarried fathers and their children is contrary to the UN Declaration on the Rights of the Child, Article 7, Paragraph 1 of which states: "The child shall be registered immediately after birth and shall have the right from birth to a name, the right to acquire a nationality and, as far as possible, the right to know and be cared for by his or her parents". Commenting on this situation, the UN Committee on the Rights of the Child – whose function is to oversee implementation of the UN Declaration on the Rights of the Child in Ireland and elsewhere - has expressed its concern about "the disadvantaged situation of children born of unmarried parents due to the lack of appropriate procedures to name the father in the birth registration of the child"[67].

It is difficult to know what effect this situation has on unmarried fathers – other than to make them feel inferior to the mother vis à vis the child – but its effects on the child are generally well known. I cite only the recorded experience of the writer Hugh Leonard who, on discovering that the stroke of a pen took the place of his father's name on the birth certificate, observed that: "If my mother had thought to invent a name for my father, my own life would certainly have been different. ... I have always been a cuckoo in any and every Irish nest. ... I say this as a simple reality"[68]. Many similar accounts bear testimony to the abiding presence of the absent father.

The exact number of children whose right to know their father is not being vindicated in this regard is difficult to estimate but in 1998 the Department of Social, Community and Family Affairs surveyed a sample of 1,000 unmarried applicants for One-Parent Family Payment and found that 79% of them had both parents names on each child's birth certificate. In other words, about 20% of the children of unmarried fathers – equivalent to around 3,000 children per annum- may never know or be able to find out – who their natural father is[69].

"The United States is rapidly moving toward the experience of several European countries in which an 'unmarried birth' is more likely to occur in a two-parent family than it is to create a mother-only family. ... a fact that has implications for how we should think about 'families' on the one hand, and 'unmarried childbearing' on the other".

LARRY BUMPASS AND HSIEN-HEN LU, 2000:6-7

---

[66] European Court of Human Rights, 1994:3.
[67] United Nations Committee on the Rights of the Child, 1998, paragraph 17, p.7; see also The Children's Right's Alliance, 1997, paragraphs 99-101, p.23.
[68] Leonard, 1995:36-38.
[69] See McKeown, 2001.

"Honour your father and your mother so that you may live long".

THE BIBLE, BOOK OF EXODUS, CH 20.

Fathers and Guardianship

Guardianship is a common law concept and essentially defines a relationship between an adult and a child such that the adult who is designated a guardian has the right to make all decisions affecting the welfare of the child such as where the child may live, who may have access to the child, how the child is brought up, what type of education it receives, the type of health care which the child may receive (such as an operation), et cetera. Guardianship also means that a child cannot be placed for adoption without the consent of the guardian, unless a court makes an order dispensing with that consent.

All married parents are automatically guardians of their children and share guardianship rights. However when married parents separate, their guardianship rights can become the subject of dispute, particularly their guardianship rights of access or custody to a child. In these instances, a District Court is empowered to decide under section 11 of the Guardianship of Infants Act, 1964 as to how the rights of custody / access / maintenance / etc., are to be divided between the parents even though they both remain guardians of their children.

Unmarried fathers do not have automatic guardianship rights to their children. Under the Status of Children Act 1987, non-marital fathers have the right to apply to the District Court for guardianship. The Children Act, 1997 provides that application to the court for guardianship is only necessary when unmarried parents fail to reach agreement. This is virtually identical to the law on granting "parental responsibility" to unmarried fathers in England and Wales under Section 4 of The Children Act 1989 where there is now official recognition that this situation is no longer acceptable: "Discrimination between married and unmarried fathers in respect of parental responsibility is increasingly seen as unacceptable, in view of the large number of children who are now born to unmarried parents, many of whom are likely to be in stable relationships. It is clearly impossible to assume that most unmarried fathers are irresponsible or uninterested in their children, and do not deserve a legal role as parents"[70].

The rights of all fathers - married, separated, divorced, unmarried - to custody and access of the children can be restricted by the courts under the Guardianship of Infants Act, 1964. These proceedings are held in private or "in camera" and accordingly, it is impossible to know how judges apportion these rights between parents. Some anecdotal evidence suggests that the Irish courts tend to weigh custody and access decisions in favour of mothers. In 1995, the Department of Social, Community and Family Affairs, replying to a Council of Europe questionnaire on the rights of fathers stated that: "In cases where parents separate, custody can be awarded to either parent. In practice, it is far more common to be awarded to the mother than the father"[71].

Fathers and the Family Law System

A large proportion of family breakdowns in Ireland - possibly as high as two thirds, depending on how one interprets data in the 1996 Census of

---

[70] Lord Chancellor's Department, 1998:15.
[71] Council of Europe, 1995:230.

Population - occur without being processed through the courts. As such, the image of family breakdown as presented through the court system represents only a subset of this reality and probably the more conflictual and acrimonious subset. Moreover since family cases are heard in private, it is impossible to know precisely how decisions are made, on what basis, and in whose favour.

Table 5.1 gives the breakdown of married and separated persons in Ireland in 1996. This reveals that around 6% of the ever-married population described themselves as separated or divorced. However only two fifths (41%) of these appear to be legally separated or divorced thus indicating that the majority of ever-married men and women involved in family break-up do not have recourse to the court system in Ireland.

Table 5.1 Marital Status of Ever-Married Men and Women in Ireland in 1996

Marital Status	Men	Women	Total
1. Total Ever Married (1)	710,616	733,789	1,444,405
2. Total Separated / Divorced	35,661	52,131	87,792
3. Deserted	6,363	16,785	23,148
4. Marriage annulled	920	1,287	2,207
5. Legally separated	11,863	14,616	26,479
6. Other separated	11,741	14,430	26,171
7. Divorced	4,774	5,013	9,787
Separated/divorced as % of ever married(2 as % of 1)	5	7	6
Legally separated/divorced as % of separated (5+7 as % of 2)	47	38	41

(1) Total ever-married includes all married, re-married and separated persons and excludes widows.
Source: Census of Population, 1996.

The family law system in Ireland performs two main functions: a protection function involving barring and protection orders and a separation function involving maintenance and guardianship. Most of the family law cases, according to one study[72], are initiated by women (85%); men and fathers (15%) are a distinct minority in terms of using the District Court to resolve family disputes. In effect this means that the family law system, as applied in practice in Ireland, is "a woman's resource rather than a man's resource"[73]. This raises the question as to why so few men use the court system to redress family grievances[74].

Guardianship is effectively the only area where fathers use the family law system to redress family disputes essentially because, unlike mothers, they do not have automatic guardianship rights. Moreover, this is the only area of the family law system where the applicant is more likely to be a man than a woman. In their study Fahey and Lyons found that the most common issue in guardianship cases coming before the Dublin Metropolitan District court was access followed by custody[75].

The traditional stereotype of the unmarried father - and to a lesser extent, the separated father - is that he is not interested in having custody of, or access to, his children. However, the apparent growth in numbers of

[72] Fahey and Lyons, 1995
[73] Fahey and Lyons, 1995:136.
[74] See McKeown and Kidd, 2000.
[75] Fahey and Lyons, 1995:29.

separated and unmarried fathers who apply for joint custody of their children seems to reflect, at least in part, a desire by these fathers to remain involved with their children. It may also reflect a fear that this involvement could be cut off unless protected by law. Commenting on the significance of joint custody cases in England - where the mother is reputedly awarded sole custody in the vast majority of cases –a social worker has observed that: "In legal terms, it might not seem that a joint custody order makes very much difference. .... However, psychologically, a joint custody order affirms the continuing role of both parents in the lives of their children. I will suggest that this is something that may have great significance for the children. A further advantage of such [joint custody] orders is that they can avoid the implication that the disposal of custody is a winner-take-all situation"[76].

In Ireland, there has been a steady increase in the number of unmarried fathers applying for guardianship custody and access over the past few years. In part, this reflects the introduction of the Status of Children Act 1987 but, at a deeper level, it may reflect a greater interest in active fathering by unmarried fathers through having their rights to guardianship, custody and access acknowledged by the court. It is true, as Table 5.2 reveals, that the number of applications for guardianship, custody and access (4,457) by unmarried fathers in 2000 was only a quarter of non-marital births (17,235) in that year; equally however it is known from one Irish study that up to half of fathers remain in relationship with the unmarried mother of their child[77], thus suggesting that legal remedies are only resorted to in a minority of cases.

Table 5.2 Applications for Guardianship, Custody and Access by Unmarried Fathers in Ireland, 2000

Type of Application	N	% of Total	% Granted	% Non-Marital Births*
Custody and Access	612	14	68	4
Custody only	623	14	61	4
Access only	2,213	50	77	13
Guardianship	1,009	22	76	6
Total	4,457	100	73	26

*The number of non-marital births in Ireland in 2000 was 17,235.
Source: Courts Service, Dublin.

Single Fathers and Social Exclusion

The reality of life for single fathers – as indeed for single mothers - is that most of them live in relatively disadvantaged circumstances; most of them have low levels of education and poor earning capacity; many of them are not able to meet the cost of independently supporting a family. Without the intervention of the State, family life in these disadvantaged communities would be virtually impossible. However the particular way in which the State intervenes to help lone mothers and fathers – and the ideologies which support this intervention - is such as to add to the social exclusion of lone fathers by effectively prohibiting cohabitation and co-parenting[78]. As a result, many lone fathers not only face exclusion from the labour market and an important source of identity and fulfilment through work, but they also face the even deeper form of social exclusion from family life and an irreplaceable stakeholding in society through parenting their children as

[76] Richards, 1982:137.
[77] Richardson, 1991:177.
[78] See McKeown, 2001.

breadwinners and homemakers. Many children in these families also suffer from not having a father living with them or even in regular contact with them.

Concluding Comment

In assessing the impact of the law on fathers, it is important to remember that the way the law is interpreted and implemented can be just as important as the letter and content of the law. This is probably as true of family law as other types of law but is more than ordinarily difficult to prove because family law cases are heard in private and complete records of proceedings are not kept, much less published. As a result, there is almost no public information on how the family law system actually works. It is known that quite a large number of fathers who have come in contact with the family law courts are dissatisfied with the operation of the system and this seems to be the case in Ireland as much as elsewhere, thereby drawing attention to the need for more transparency and research in this area.

Beyond the courts, the law can have deeply practical implications even to the point of defining which family members can have access to family support services. All services to families, with rare exceptions, can only work with the consent of the legal parents or guardians of children since to do otherwise would be unethical and illegal. In many instances this effectively excludes single fathers and makes mothers the gatekeepers to services for these fathers[79]. In these cases, the law's definition of family membership has the further consequence of regulating who, within each family, can or cannot receive family support services.

[79] See Kane, 2001:76

How Do Non-Resident Fathers Parent Their Children?

"The evidence from our experience seems to suggest that some fathers genuinely wish to be involved with their children, they want their children to know them, to spend time with them and to experience their extended family. However our evidence also suggests that there are major obstacles in the way of some fathers in having a relationship with their children born outside marriage"

MARGARET DROMEY AND MARGOT DOHERTY, TREOIR: FEDERATION OF SERVICES FOR UNMARRIED PARENTS AND THEIR CHILDREN, 1992:11

The term "non-resident" father is used to denote the reality of those fathers who, for whatever reason, do not live with their children. Fathers in such circumstances typically experience more difficulty in parenting their children compared to resident fathers. Research on non-resident fathers has tended to focus on two aspects of the parenting relationship: the frequency of contact and the payment of maintenance. Of course neither measures, on their own, tell us much about impact on the well-being of children or indeed the well-being of non-resident fathers which results from such parenting[80].

We begin by looking at contact between non-resident fathers and their children. A major study on contact between non-resident fathers and their children was undertaken in Britain in 1995 / 1996 by a team of researchers at the University of York. This study, based on interviews with over 600 non-resident fathers, found that nearly half (47%) were in contact with their children at least once a week and two thirds (68%) were in contact at least once a month; conversely, a fifth (21%) had not seen their children in the past year[81]. There is no comparable data in Ireland although a longitudinal study of non-marital births at the National Maternity Hospital in Dublin between 1986 and 1989 found that half the single parents were in a stable relationship with each other at the time of the child's birth[82] while, one year later, half of the fathers shared some of the parenting role with the mother[83]. Conversely, in the US about 40%-50% of non-resident fathers seem to lose contact with their children[84]. All of these studies suggest a significant level of contact between non-resident fathers and their children in at least half of all cases.

Given the potential benefits of contact between non-resident fathers and their children[85] it is appropriate to examine the factors which influence the level of contact. In the British study, two sets of factors were identified as key determinants. The first is relationship with the mother: "fathers who had an amicable relationship with the mother were much more likely to have regular contact with the child than those whose relationship with the mother was hostile"[86] The second is socio-economic characteristics: "the best-fitting model selected four variables which contribute to the odds of a father having regular contact – being in employment, living close, having only one child, and living in a household without children"[87].

[80] Other aspects of parenting by non-resident fathers include informal supports for children such as pocket money, presents, holiday, shoes, clothing, etc. A British survey of over 600 non-resident fathers in 1995 /1996 found that 86% gave some form of informal support (Bradshaw, Stimson, Skinner and Williams, 1999a:156).
[81] The authors point out that the level of contact reported by non-resident fathers is considerably higher than that reported by resident mothers in one parent households in an earlier survey (Bradshaw and Miller, 1991). This is not that unusual however and is one of the difficulties associated with research involving couples and families since men and women in family relationships perceive themselves and their contribution to the family differently (see for example Marsiglio, 1995; Hawkins, Christiansen, Pond Sargent and Hill, 1995; O'Leary and Arias, 1988).
[82] Flanagan and Richardson, 1992:83
[83] Richardson and Kernan, 1992:83
[84] Furstenberg and Cherlin, 1991:35-36; Seltzer, 2000:55
[85] The benefits of contact between children and their fathers – both resident and non-resident – is likely to depend on what happens during that contact. For a creative guide to ways in which fathers, and indeed mothers, can spend time with their children, see Carroll, 2000
[86] Bradshaw, Stimson, Skinner and Williams, 1999b:415. It is interesting and appropriate to note that "seventy-one per cent of the fathers said that they still had some contact with the mothers of their children. About half of those with contact (49 per cent) described their relationship with their former partner as amicable, another quarter as amicable but distant. Only 18 per cent described the relationship as "distant and hostile, hostile or non-existent" (Bradshaw, Stimson, Skinner and Williams, 1999a:87). On the basis of regression analysis, the authors discovered that "new children and new step-children may result in a deterioration in relationships with former partners, and compete for time and attention with the absent children" (ibid).
[87] ibid:413

The importance of relationship with the mother also emerged in the Dublin study of non-marital births which found that the mother's attitude to parenting was improved by contact with the non-resident father[88]. Staff in Treoir, the Federation of Services for Unmarried Parents are also of the view, based on their contacts with single fathers and mothers, that mothers are effectively the gatekeepers to contact between non-resident fathers and their children and access can be undermined or denied in three ways[89]: (1) where the child is given no information about the father and his name may not even by registered on his birth certificate (2) where the child is given only negative information about the father and (3) where access is denied or severely limited if the relationship with the mother breaks down or the mother enters a new relationship.

We now turn to the payment of maintenance by non-resident fathers. In Ireland, the proportion of one parent households in receipt of maintenance from non-resident fathers, where the household is also in receipt of the One-Parent Family Payment, is about 20% in the case of single parents and 30% in the case of separated and divorced parents[90]. In the UK, the corresponding figure is around 30% of one parent households[91]. Studies from the US suggest a higher level of payment with 52% of non-resident fathers paying at least some maintenance compared to 39% of divorced non-resident mothers[92].

One of the fundamental issues affecting the payment of maintenance is the perceived legitimacy of the arrangement, particularly in the highly charged context where non-resident fathers are expected to pay maintenance while access to the children may be restricted by the mother. The study of non-resident fathers in Britain is particularly useful in highlighting how the perceived legitimacy of the maintenance arrangements, and the manner in which they are negotiated, are crucial in determining if those arrangements are honoured by non-resident fathers. According to this study, "the mother's right to claim maintenance on behalf of the children was accepted if she at least recognised, if not actively supported, the father's independent relationship with his child(ren). If the mothers failed to accept the father-child relationship or failed to sustain it through granting contact, then the fathers found this extremely difficult to comprehend. ... The resulting attitudes tended to be that there was no point in paying maintenance as the children would not know their fathers were supporting them"[93]. The importance of maintenance arrangements which are legitimised in the context of joint parenting was also underlined by the Commission on the Family: "The Commission considers that realising the potential of improving income for lone parents through adequate maintenance arrangements for children, has to be part of a longer-term strategy involving the promotion of responsible joint parenting by young women and men which is desirable in their child's interest"[94]

In addition to issues of legitimacy, there are often very practical considerations which affect the payment of maintenance. By far the most important consideration is the father's ability to pay as measured by income and employment status. In the British study, the authors found that non-

"If noncustodial parents are to maintain and strengthen relationships with their children ... they need to participate in a range of everyday activities that allow them to function as parents rather than simply as regular, genial visitors"

MICHAEL LAMB, 1999:117.

---

88 Richardson and Kernan, 1992: 83.
89 see Dromey and Doherty, 1992
90 See Department of Social, Community and Family Affairs, 2000:107-108
91 Bradshaw and Millar, 1991
92 Sorensen and Zibman, 2000; see also Seltzer, 2000:55; Meyer, 1999:139-140
93 Bradshaw, Stimson, Skinner and Williams, 1999b:424.

"Joint custody and divorce mediation seem to be the most effective methods of maintaining involvement of the nonresident parent and sustaining child support."

MAVIS HETHERINGTON AND MARGARET STANLEY-HAGEN, 1997:210.

resident fathers who were unemployed were 20 times less likely to pay maintenance than employed fathers[95]. The same result has also been replicated in a number of US studies[96]. The British study also found that younger fathers who had lost contact with the mother were less likely to pay although this finding is not replicated in US studies[97]. These findings suggest that, at least for low income non-resident fathers, measures to improve their employment and earnings, in conjunction with measures to improve family relationships, may have a more beneficial impact on the payment of maintenance than stricter enforcement.

The way in which non-resident fathers parent their children – and are supported to do so – is likely to remain a salient issue for the foreseeable future as marital breakdown and births outside marriage remain at current or even higher levels. In this chapter we have reviewed how the fathering role gets expressed through contact and maintenance but, to some extent, these arrangements fall far short of what it is to be a father or a parent generally and this, in turn, may account for why some non-resident fathers lose contact with their children. The typical scenario facing many non-resident fathers is graphically illustrated by one researcher in the following terms: "Most noncustodial parents are awarded visitation and they function as visitors, taking their children to the zoo, to movies, to dinner, and to other special activities in much the same way that grandparents or uncles and aunts behave. Children may well enjoy these excursions, and may not regret the respite from arguments about completing homework, cleaning up their rooms, behaving politely, having their hair cut (or not having their hair cut!), going to bed on time, getting ready for school, and respecting their siblings' property and their parents' limited resources, but the exclusion of fathers from these everyday tribulations is crucial, ultimately transforming the fathers' roles and making these men increasingly irrelevant to their children's lives, socialisation, and development. Many men describe this as a sufficiently painful experience that they feel excluded from and pushed out of their children's lives"[98].

It is considerations such as these which point to the importance of joint parenting in order to support the parenting role of non-resident fathers, especially those fathers who, by virtue of their economic and legal status, are at greatest risk of being excluded from their children and a stakeholding in family life. The precise way in which joint parenting is arranged, and the possibility of supporting joint legal custody through joint physical custody is a challenging issue requiring great sensitivity to ensure that the well-being of everyone in this type of family (mother, father and child) is safeguarded and promoted.

---

[94] Commission on the Family, 1998:115. Some of the difficulties which arise in this regard in Ireland are illustrated dramatically in a recent study which found that young single mothers would prefer not to accept maintenance since "if the father paid maintenance this would undermine their ability to control access and to protect their children(as they saw it)" (Russell and Corcoran, 2000:17). These mothers would prefer the State to deduct maintenance straight from earnings or benefits "as a way of ensuring the payment was more regular and of avoiding contact with an ex-partner" (ibid:18). Perhaps even more discouraging is the fact that the study erroneously interprets these findings as providing "support for the DSCFA taking a more active role in pursuing the absent parent for maintenance and for collecting such payments" (ibid:19). Such an interpretation is quite at variance with the views of the Commission on the Family and, if the experience of the Child Support Agency in Britain is any guide, would further damage relationships in these fragile families. It is not without good reason that social policy analysts have described the Child Support Agency in Britain as "the worst policy-making disaster in modern British history" (Bradshaw, Stimson, Skinner and Williams, 1999b:416).
[95] Bradshaw, Stimson, Skinner and Williams, 1999b:Table 17.6, pp.419-420
[96] Garfinkel and Klawitter, 1990; Sonenstein and Calhoun, 1990; Nichols-Casebolt and Danzinger, 1989; Peters, Argys, Maccoby and Mnookin, 1993; Meyer, 1999.
[97] ibid
[98] Lamb, 1999.

The term "stepfamily" refers to families which are created when a parent takes a new partner, whether through marriage or cohabitation[99]. This term covers a wide range of situations from where a non-biological parent – usually a man – may have been a parent figure in a child's life since it was a baby through to situations involving a series of brief cohabitations over a number of years. This diversity draws attention to the heterogeneity of stepfamilies and has led one group of researchers to suggest that "any attempt to describe stepfamilies as if they were one single discrete and definable family form is highly misleading and limiting"[100].

The reality is that the number of stepfamilies, in whatever form they take, is on the increase and is part and parcel of the growing process of breakdown and reconstitution among families. Countries such as the US, UK and Australia where up to 50% of first marriages end in divorce have growing proportions of stepfamilies. In the US, for example, it is estimated that 11% of children live with a stepparent, most commonly a stepfather[101]. In Ireland the number of people in the Census of Population who describe themselves as "remarried following the dissolution of a previous marriage" trebled in the ten years between 1986 and 1996; not all of these remarriages result in stepfamilies but some undoubtedly do while other stepfamilies are formed outside of marriage altogether. Thus stepfamilies can take a variety of legal forms.

A crucial question in the present context concerns the impact which stepfathers have on the well-being of children. One of the obvious benefits of stepfathers is that they normally increase household income which improves the children's standard of living[102]. Paradoxically, the entry of a stepfather can also have the effect of diminishing the role of non-resident biological fathers. This is suggested by research in the UK which found that non-resident fathers tended to have less contact with their biological children if they were in a second relationship and living with stepchildren[103]. This highlights a more general feature of stepfamily life: "The pressures of stepfamily life for both adults and children are greater than in nuclear or even lone parent families, and many stepfathers who also have their own children from a previous relationship may be faced with confusing emotional and financial loyalties"[104].

Despite improvements in material well-being associated with stepfathers, the research suggests that other forms of child well-being, notably psychological and behavioural adjustment, are not improved by the presence of a stepparent, either stepfather or stepmother. According to one review: "children in stepfamilies are no better off, on average, than children in divorced, single-parent families; indeed they are worse off in some respects"[105].

The main reason why stepfamilies do not improve the well-being of children – which may have been impaired by previous experiences of family life – seems to be due to the fact that relations between stepparents and stepchildren are not always close or even friendly. Some preadolescent boys

How Do Stepfathers Parent Their Children?

"Stepfathering, which is as prone to negative stereotypes as is stepmothering, is increasingly common and increasingly complex."

KYLE D. PRUETT, 1993:49.

---

99 Bornat, Dimmock, Jones and Peace, 1999:251.
100 Gorrel Barnes, Thompson, Daniel, and Burchardt, 1998:271.
101 Emery, 1999:6.
102 Teachman and Paasch, 1994.
103 Bradshaw, Stimson, Skinner and Williams, 1999b:415.
104 Burgess and Ruxton, 1996:70.
105 Amato, 1999:169.

"Shared parenting is generally the best situation for most children post separation".

JOHN SHARRY, PETER REID AND EUGENE DONOHOE, 2001:3.

Step-fathers often become more involved in domestic life than biological fathers. This may be because parents in blended families realise the mistakes that were made first time round or it may be because they are older and have more time."

CHARLIE LEWIS AND JO WARIN, 2001:8.

have been found to respond positively to the introduction of a stepfather although adolescents of both genders are likely to react negatively[106]. Many children view the stepfather as an outsider, reject the stepfather's attempts to exert authority, and are jealous of the emotional bond between stepfather and the mother[107]. Stepmothers experience even more difficulty than stepfathers in this regard[108]. At the same time, stepfathers often become more involved in parenting than biological fathers: "research suggests that stepfathers may be more attentive to the needs of their children and that they are less arbitrary in their parenting style than are fathers of many intact families, partly because their consciousness has been raised about the overriding significance of two parents in the lives of their children"[109]

One synthesis of the research suggests that the well-being of stepfamilies is affected by the following factors: "Factors that aggravate the stepfamily situation include continued conflict between the biological parents, less acceptance of parental authority, copying of inter-parental discord witnessed before divorce and disengagement by mothers and stepfathers, with a decrease in parental monitoring of adolescents"[110].

Despite the general difficulties experienced by stepfathers, and stepfamilies generally, there is also evidence that when relations between stepparents and stepchildren are close, children appear to benefit. For example one US study found that children have higher school grades when stepfathers help with homework, attend school events, and are in other ways involved in school activities[111]. Another study found that a close relationship with stepfathers is associated with enhanced psychological well-being among young adults[112]. These findings indicate that stepfathers (and presumably stepmothers) have the potential to be important resources for children even if this potential is often unmet.

Aside from the immediate impact of stepparents on children, we know relatively little about the role of extended stepfamilies in the lives of children and the type and levels of support which these may offer. Extended stepfamilies are sources of support but they tend to be less supportive than traditional kin networks of never-divorced parents. That is the conclusion of one review of the research which found that extended stepfamily relationships involve "weak rather than strong ties"[113].

Overall, the evidence on stepfathers, and stepfamilies generally, suggests that they are likely to be more vulnerable than conventional two parent families, particularly in terms of relational well-being and its associated benefits. Some of these vulnerabilities, particularly in the case of children, arise as much from the breakdown of their first family as from the reconstitution of their second. As one recent review of the literature suggested: "It may be that levels of conflict in children's first families have more to do with their well-being in stepfamilies than with what happens later"[114]. In Ireland, as elsewhere, the needs of these families require careful and sensitive consideration and new policies and practices may have to be devised to promote their well-being.

[106] Hetherington and Jodl, 1994.
[107] Hetherington and Clingempeel, 1992.
[108] Buchanan, Maccoby and Dornbusch, 1996; Hetherington and Jodl, 1994.
[109] Pruett, 1993:49.
[110] Clare, 2000:147.
[111] Bogenschneider, 1997.
[112] Amato, 1994a; see also Amato, 1994b.
[113] Amato, 1999:171.
114 Harold, Pryor and Reynolds, 2001:5.

The predominant focus of services for families is on mothers rather than fathers; as one reviewer put it, family support is characterised by "the predominant focus on mothers and the apparent invisibility of fathers"[115]. There is a good deal of research and practice to suggest that fathers tend to be avoided by professionals – and possibly vice versa – and there is great uncertainty among professionals about how to approach fathers and work with them[116]. In social work as in family support, parenting is often treated as synonymous with mothering and tends to "filter out fathers"[117]. The reality, as many commentators have noted, is that there are virtually no strategies and interventions to involve and support fathers[118].

The way in which services are organised around families and the predominant focus on mothers is itself a reflection of the traditional division of labour in families where mothers are still the main carers of children; but they are not the only carers and fathers increasingly expect and are expected to become involved in the care of their children. However services are often slow to adapt to the changing realities of family life and even slower to take an active role in promoting change. Typically, women seem to be more willing than men to ask for help when family problems arise, irrespective of whether the problems are with their partner or with their child. At the same time, services often accept the lack of involvement of men without question and often unwittingly promote it by failing to collect information – from fathers or mothers – about the role of the father in the family thereby rendering men invisible in the family support system[119]. In other words, the low uptake of family services by men may be due as much to the way those services are designed and delivered as to any inherent reluctance on the part of men to use services generally. As one review of the research concluded: "reluctance among men to discuss problems in their parenting or relationships are compounded by the fact that the services on offer in family centres are often aimed at mothers to the exclusion of fathers"[120].

It is true that services to families reflect the broader social and cultural context in which they operate. At the same time, the design and delivery of services has an independent effect on how those services are used and by whom. This was amply revealed in a study of family centres in England and Wales which found that one of the main reasons why so few fathers used the centres was that few of the centres wanted fathers to attend or had any strategy for doing so. The research found that centres which were open to supporting fathers, irrespective of the specific strategy adopted, were more likely to get fathers involved[121]. This study also found that family centres had different ways of working with mothers and fathers such that work with women tended to follow a family-focused model in which women's needs as mothers, and as women in their own right, were acknowledged while work with fathers tended to be more child-focused, with an emphasis on childcare and little that catered on fathers' other, wider interests. The authors of this study made a number of recommendations for making family centres more open to fathers including:

How Can Family Services Support Fathers?

"The absence of men from family support services and the need to make services more accessible and acceptable to fathers has become an area of growing concern for policy makers and practitioners alike".

DEBORAH GHATE, CATHERINE SHAW AND NEAL HAZEL, 2000:2.

---

[115] Roberts and Macdonald, 1999:63; see also French, 1998:187–188; 1995; Murphy, 1996:95; Bernard Van Leer Foundation, 2001:3.
[116] see McKeown, Ferguson and Rooney, 1998, Chapter Seven
[117] Buckley, 1998.
[118] See, for example, French, 1998:187–188; see also Rylands, 1995; Murphy, 1996:95.
[119] See Kane, 2001.
[120] Lewis, 2000:6.
[121] Ghate, Shaw and Hazel, 2000.

- make a positive commitment to recruit fathers, backed up with pro-active and persistent strategies that reach out beyond the centre itself;
- work at better promotion of the centre's activities that stresses the inclusive nature of the service as a place for both parents, not just mothers and avoid negative attitudes towards men;
- reconsider the range and type of activities on offer, so that activities appeal to men as well as women;
- do not rely on men's groups as the only activity catering to men – they do not have universal appeal to men who are new to family support services.

Not all fathers are equally vulnerable and some – notably unemployed fathers, young fathers, single fathers, cohabiting fathers, non-resident fathers, and step-fathers – are clearly more vulnerable than others. Perhaps the most vulnerable are those which have a number of risk factors such as those fathers who are young, single, non-resident and unemployed; these fathers have few financial resources to bring to family life. We know that many of the young men in prison (about 70%)[122] are single, unemployed fathers although none of the services for these men acknowledges their parenting status; by contrast, prison authorities explicitly take the parenting status of women into account and every effort is made to sustain links between mothers and their children[123]. Similarly the majority of drug users in Ireland tend to be young single fathers[124] yet few services explicitly address their needs and responsibilities as parents.

There is now a growing recognition that services need to be developed to support fathers as part of a broader strategy of promoting the well-being children and families, indeed the well-being of men and women. Some organisations in the voluntary sector have taken a lead in this regard. In the US, for example, the Ford Foundation has funded programmes such as the Strengthening Families Initiative and the Fatherhood Project which have a specific focus on supporting the active involvement of men in the care of their children[125]. Similarly, the Bernard Van Leer Foundation has been funding fatherhood projects for a number of years in both the developed and developing world[126]. In Britain, Working With Men[127] and Fathers Direct[128] support the development of work with men and fathers through training, consultancy, advice, publications and resources. In Ireland, funding has been made available for men's groups since 1994;[129] these are mainly self-help groups, many of them organised around issues of personal development and the difficulties experienced as single or separated fathers. However these groups are limited in the support which they can offer each other, itself reflecting the absence of a broader network of supportive services for fathers, particularly for those living in disadvantaged circumstances.

A range of initiatives have been tried and tested in working with vulnerable fathers. In the US, for example, an organisation called NPCL (National Center for Strategic Nonprofit Planning and Community Leadership)[130] has

---

[122] O'Mahony, 1997:37-8.
[123] McKeown, 2001.
[124] McKeown and Fitzgerald, 1999; McKeown, Fitzgerald and Deehan, 1993.
[125] www.fordfound.org
[126] Bernard Van Leer Foundation, 2001.
[127] Working With Men is a non-for-profit organisation founded in 1988. See Working With Men, 1999; see also Roker, Richardson and Coleman, 2000:32-35. Website: www.wwm.uk.freeuk.com
[128] Fathers Direct was established in 1999 as the national information centre for fatherhood in the UK; it is funded by public and private grants. Website: www.fathersdirect.com
[129] Cousins, 1997.
[130] NPCL is based in Washington DC. Website: www.npcl.org

used funding from the Ford foundation to develop a 25 session programme for vulnerable fathers which involves facilitated discussion of the following topics: (1) personal development (team building and discussion of values, manhood and self-sufficiency); (2) life skills (communication, dealing with stress and coping with discrimination); (3) responsible fatherhood (covering roles and responsibilities of fatherhood, child development, a father's impact on his children, how to be a positive influence, handling the daily needs of children, effective discipline, negotiating the child support enforcement system, etc.); (4) relationships (effective communication, managing anger, resolving conflicts and negotiating relationships); (5) health and sexuality (taking charge of your health, understanding sexuality, dealing with substance abuse, reducing sexual risks). In addition, NPCL runs training courses and other support services for the facilitators on these programmes.

In Britain, NEWPIN have been running fathers groups since 1997, drawing upon their experience of running mothers groups[131]. Its 32 week programme is designed to help men learn the value of themselves and their importance to children and to appraise relationships with the mothers of their children even though these may have broken down or are conflictual. The programme involves a group seminar and facilitated discussion as well as individual sessions, weekends with their children and shared meals. NEWPIN has also developed a Community Fathers programme so that fathers who have been through its programme can act as volunteer support persons to other fathers who are experiencing difficulties.

In Ireland, Barnardos developed a mens' group and a womens' group as an integral part of its family support programme in Moyross, Limerick where therapeutic work with individuals and families was complemented by group work processes[132]. Fathers were recruited to join the project through a community-based soccer tournament after conventional open-days proved ineffective. As elsewhere, the fathers' group moved from a focus on activities to a focus on discussion of men's roles as parents and partners as well as their health and lifestyles. This process led to the emergence of a cohesive group which had discernible benefits for the fathers and their families[133]. Also in Ireland, Cherish have been running parenting courses for unmarried fathers since 2000.

The development of services for fathers faces a number of specific challenges including:
- Finding out the needs of fathers, particularly the needs of different types of vulnerable fathers, and the most appropriate types of service response; it is worth reflecting that the low uptake of existing services by fathers may itself be an indication that many of these services are inappropriate.
- Adopting and promoting a strengths-based perspective to work with fathers as with families generally; too often, it would appear, fathers are seen by professionals from a negative deficit perspective rather than as persons with needs and strengths.

---

[131] NEWPIN was established in 1980 to break the cycle of destructive family behaviour and has 14 centres throughout the UK. Its Fathers' Centre was established in London in 1997 to help men build stronger relationships with their children and their communities. Email: fathers@nationalnewpin.freeserve.co.uk See also Lloyd, 2001:46-52

[132] Jones, 1998.

[133] Personal communication with Blaire McClure who worked on the project; see also Jones, 1998:22.

- Training professionals to see fathers as part of the family even where they are not living in the same household as the mother and child; it is no longer valid to assume that the household and the family are the same thing given the extent of marital breakdown and of births outside marriage.
- Recruiting more men into the caring professions so that services to families are seen as the business of men as much as women; this does not imply that only men can only work with men but it does suggest that the work of caring, both inside and outside the family, is an appropriate calling for both men and women and this is not reflected in the current gender-imbalance in the caring professions.
- Promoting awareness of family services in a way which is seen as supportive of men and fathers at every stage of the life cycle from child birth to old age; many of the existing images of family services focus primarily on the mother and child.

The practicalities of making family services more inclusive of fathers is a major challenge. Research on best practice in this area suggests that two key stages are involved[134]. The first involves an audit of existing attitudes among management, staff and parents within the service to the involvement of fathers by asking at least two key questions: (1) are you in favour of involving fathers in the service? and (2) what would the service look like if it was more inclusive of fathers? The second stage involves developing a concrete strategy for father involvement which involves the following key steps: (1) creating a father-friendly environment within the service by encouraging fathers to become involved, finding out what they want, recognising and addressing the fears of fathers as well as mothers and staff, displaying positive images of fatherhood in the centre, etc; (2) recruiting men to work in the service, both as staff and volunteers; (3) designing and delivering programmes of shared and separate activities for fathers, mothers and children as appropriate; (4) sustain fathers' involvement through positive feedback, regular reviews of progress, cultivating leadership and building networks. Ideally, all of these activities should be informed by an attitude of tailoring the service to meet the needs of fathers and families generally rather than the reverse.

A useful checklist by which a service can audit its accessibility to men and fathers is contained in Table 8.1. This audit is a valuable exercise for all services but particularly those involved in family support services.

Developing services for fathers is inextricably linked to the broader context of promoting the material and relational well-being of families since that is a fundamental goal of family policy[135]. Fathers and families who are vulnerable as a result of poverty, conflict or instability are most likely to need the support of family services. At the same time, the efficacy of these services necessarily depends on the broader structural supports in society which promote family well-being. In practice this means that family services need to be complemented by a larger range of policy measures which actively support joint parenting irrespective of the marital or residential status of parents as well as measures to ensure that families do not live in poverty. In short, the goal of supporting fathers needs to be seen as integral to the promotion of family well-being, not an optional extra.

---

134 See Levine, Murphy, and Wilson, 1998; Levine and Pitt, 1995; Burgess and Ruxton, 1996.
135 McKeown and Sweeney, 2001.

Table 8.1 Checklist for Auditing the Accessibility of a Service to Men and Fathers

Walls and Notice Boards
- Are images of men displayed?
- Are there leaflets, posters and other materials relevant to men available?

Leaflets, Posters and Brochures
- Do the images and text say men are welcome here?
- Are letters addressed to both parents where the service involves children?

Assessing Men's Involvement
- Are men involved as clients or patients in clinics, groups or education sessions you facilitate?
- Are men actively and continually encouraged to participate?

Staff Attitudes
- Do you relate differently to men and women clients / patients?
- Do you feel more comfortable approaching women than men?
- Do you assume men positively want to be involved?
- Do you expect men will be interested in their children's health?
- If a mother and father are present with a child, do you listen and talk to both of them?
- Do you value his contribution?
- Do you schedule your visits or appointments to suit both parents?

Recruiting Men
- Do you want men to be involved?
- Are you prepared to make the first contact?
- Can you enlist other local health or community professionals to help with recruitment?
- Can women clients be encouraged to help recruit men?
- Can you ask male clients known to you to approach other men?
- Is providing help specifically for men possible in your work context?
- Can you tap into work, trade union, sports, fitness or leisure networks?

Source: Robertson and Williams, 1998:288.

9

Can Fathering Skills Be Taught?

"Becoming a father, that is simple. Being one is hard"

MIKE LILLEY, 1997:13.

Parenting, whether by mothers or fathers, is much more than a skill. It is a way of being a person and of being in relationship. This is worth affirming in view of the tendency to see parenting problems as essentially as "skill deficits" which can be rectified by imparting techniques. Techniques may indeed help but only if they help parents to develop as persons and to form healthy relationships with the child.

The focus on the skill aspects of parenting, whether by fathers or mothers, has some dangers which are worth alluding to. The first, which has already been mentioned in Chapter Four, is that it may, however unintentionally, place all the responsibility for child well-being on the parent-child relationship while ignoring the findings of research which suggest that the parent-parent relationship may be just as important. Second, the emphasis on skills carries the danger of subtle authoritarianism which allows experts to tell parents how to rear their children given that skill – as opposed to art - implies certainty about how something is to be done. It is useful to bear these dangers in mind since, without appropriate reflection, the emphasis on parenting skills can effectively undermine parents and fail to properly respect the natural diversity in the way that parents rear their children. These reflections seem particularly appropriate in the context of fathers since the negative stereotypes which seem to inform much thinking about men and fathers typically lead to programmes on how to fix the stereotype rather than address their expressed needs as persons.

An essential starting point therefore in discussing the question of whether fathering skills can be taught is to recognise that being a good father is essentially a derivative of being a "good man" in the same way that a good mother is inseparable from a good woman. Each is called, by virtue of his existence, to discover what it is, uniquely, to be a good man. A good man, in this sense, will always be a good father. The reverse process - of presenting fathering as the raison d'être of a man's existence - carries the danger that a father's purpose in life becomes substituted for his child's purpose in life. The implications of this, which apply equally well to mothers, have been starkly highlighted by one psychologist as follows: "I have learned, through years of work with patients and in men's retreats, and from listening to what cautions me, that when a child substitutes for your daimon you will resent that child, even grow to hate it, despite good will and high ethics. .... . When your child becomes the reason for your life, you have abandoned the invisible reason you are here. ... . Any father who has abandoned the small voice of his unique genius, turning it over to the small child he has fathered, cannot bear reminders of what he has neglected. .... . Result: a child-dominated fatherless culture with dysfunctional children"[136].

The question of how best to father children also needs to recognise that the way in which men play the role of father inevitably varies widely according to their own experiences of being men and of being fathered, their marital and residential status, the number and ages of their children, their social class and employment status, and the relative importance which they attribute - consciously or unconsciously - to work and to fathering and to seeing fathering as valuable work. Inevitably, in view of such complexity, there are many ways to be a good father just as there are many ways to be a good

---

[136]Hillman, 1996:83-85.

mother. Parenting skills need to build on this diversity and respect rather than erase it.

In trying to define what is a "good enough" father, I have come to the somewhat minimalist conclusion that the good enough father must be physically present on a reasonably regular basis to his child and have a positive rather than a negative influence on his child. A positive influence is not so easy to define although it certainly involves protecting the child from harm through a bond of attachment with the child. Beyond that, as one psychiatrist at the Tavistock Clinic in London has pointed out, "we need to be careful not to be too certain about what we think is right for children. ... the truth is that there are no rules about child care but there are some principles that we can be fairly confident are universal"[137]. The most important of these principles, according to the same psychiatrist, is attachment which is taken to mean protection from physical and emotional harm: "A secure attachment is like an invisible elastic which can stretch and contract depending on the need for protection. So when you are ill or in pain, tired or afraid, you move towards the person with whom you feel secure and when all is well you can move away to explore the world around. Clearly this applies to all of us, but most of all to small children"[138].

The importance of attachment and the associated flexibility which allows both closeness and distance has also been emphasised by other commentators: "A father who is too close or too remote will not be good enough. ... In contrast, the good father is able to successfully maintain the golden mean. Such a father is close but not too close, strong but not overwhelming, loving but not seductive, supportive but able to discipline, caring but encouraging autonomy"[139].

I have already expressed some reservations about the dangers of being too prescriptive in terms of telling parents how to bring up their children. However if these reservations are borne in mind, some practical guidelines can be a useful basis for inviting parents to reflect on how they interact with their children. In this spirit, I conclude by offering the following "Six Ways to be a Better Dad!", as summarised in Table 9.1, which might form a basis for helping fathers to reflect on fathering.

"If children were simply satisfied with what the parents offered to them, they would remain children forever. It's not simply that parents don't try to give enough to the child, rather it's that whatever the parents give is never enough for the child. The child has a destiny outside the imagination of the parents. The child has an origin that is not simply made of the understanding of its parents. There is a mysterious occurrence when the child is born.".

MICHAEL MEADE, 1993:67

---

[137] Kraemer, 1995:14.
[138] Ibid.
[139] Abramovitch, 1997:31.

Table 9.1 Six Ways to be a Better Dad

1. BEING A ROLE MODEL

As a dad, you are a role model whether you realise it or not. How you act teaches your kids how to act when they grow up. For example, if you talk problems through, your kids will probably grow up to do the same. If you lose your temper, get abusive or become violent, your kids will probably grow up to do the same.
- Kids learn mainly from what you do, not what you say.
- Treat your daughter with love and respect so she grows up expecting to be treated the same by boys and men.
- Teach your son that a man is caring, fair, a mate to his kids and treats women with respect.

2. SHOW THEM YOU CARE

Getting involved in your kids' lives is a terrific way to show your kids you care.
- Do things that they want you to do.
- Give them a hug and tell them they're great.
- Help out with their homework.
- Play footy or basketball.
- Go to a school function, go to parent / teacher interviews, watch them play sport.
- Learn their friends and teachers names.

3. WORK AND FAMILY

Let's face it, work can be tiring, stressful, and create worries. No doubt these worries are for real, but it isn't fair or useful to pass them on to your kids.
- Put aside some time just for you to recharge your batteries.
- Look after your health through diet and exercise.
- Try and leave your work hassles at work.

4. WHAT TO DO WHEN YOUR KID'S BEHAVIOUR IS NOT O.K.
- As hard as it is, try and stay calm!
- When you feel stressed and feel that you might lash out - walk away.
- Leave the room and do something to distract yourself.
- Don't act in anger or you will probably regret what you do.
- Kids need to learn right from wrong. Set rules and stick to them. Be clear about what will happen when the rules are broken. This could include not letting your kids watch their favourite TV program. If they break the rules, do what you said would happen.

5. PARENTING AND PARTNERSHIPS

Being a parent is a partnership - whether you and your children's mother are together or not.
- Respect your kid's mother.
- Don't argue in front of the kids.
- Do something about relationship problems.
- Get professional advice if you can't sort out problems together.
- Kids can't cope with their parents putting each other down.

6. SPEND TIME WITH YOUR KIDS

The time you spend with your kids is a good investment in their future. Show your love by getting involved with their sports or hobbies or involving them in your interests. Kids grow up so quickly, so don't miss out!
- Share a regular meal.
- Talk to your kids.
- Listen to their views without criticising.
- Praise their efforts.
- Encourage them and help them make decisions.

Source: The Office for Families and Children, Southern Australia.

Summary

The report is based on a reflective reading of the growing body of research which has emerged on the theme of fathers over the past decade or so. The report is organised into nine chapters each of which addresses a key question about fathers as follows. We now summarise our answers to these nine questions.

1. Why a report on fathers?

The report is written to promote understanding and appreciation of the role of fathers in family life. It is curious that such a report needs to be written but the evidence in the report itself shows that it does. One of Ireland's leading clinical psychologists who has spent a lifetime working with troubled families and children, when invited to reflect on his concerns and hopes for children in the new millennium, wrote: "First concern: the retreat of the father in Ireland as in the western world. My corresponding hope is that men will figure more and more centrally in families. ... Does anyone really believe that children are better off without a father? ... If we seek a better deal for every Irish child in the third millennium, the difference will be found largely in the quality of fathering"[140].

The growing interest in the role of fathers within families is shaped by a number of factors including the diversification of family forms such as two parent families based on cohabitation and remarriage as well as one parent families constituted through divorce and births outside marriage, the effect of which is to create a typology of fathers – single fathers, non-resident fathers, step-fathers, etc. – having varying levels of involvement with their children and equally varying legal rights and social supports for that involvement. In addition, the relationship between families and work is changing such that fathers are no longer the sole providers in the majority of families which itself has created the expectation that since mothers and fathers share the breadwinning role they should also share the childcare role within families. Beyond these factors there is also a growing appreciation, supported by research, of the significance which fathers have in the lives of children as well as the value which involved fathering has for fathers as well as mothers.

These considerations have led to the writing of this report, itself part of a growing body of writing on the general theme of fatherhood[141]. In addition to promoting understanding and appreciation, the purpose of the report is also to stimulate action in areas where the positive involvement of fathers in the lives of their children is at risk or insufficiently supported. Such an agenda for action is not just for fathers; it is also for children and their mothers and for the promotion of family well-being in whatever form the family takes[142]

---

[140]Andrews, 2000. Paul Andrews, SJ is a child psychologist in private practice and former Director of St. Declan's Child Guidance Clinic. He is the author of the book Changing Children: Living with a New Generation (Andrews, 1994) as well as numerous articles.

[141]In addition to the growing corpus of reports, books and articles on fathers, there is also a plethora of valuable websites on the topic which can be accessed using "father" as the search word. One report has estimated that 700 research papers are produced annually on the theme of fathers (Lewis and Warin, 2001:1).

[142]See McKeown and Sweeney, 2001

2. Is the role of fathers changing?

The traditional model of the family in Ireland, where two parents live together with their children and where the father is the sole breadwinner, is still the norm for around half of all families. However, nearly four out of ten Irish families have two parents working while more than a tenth live in one parent households.

More than anything else, work has become the main factor impacting on families and the parenting roles of men and women. This is evident in the growing involvement of mothers in the labour force whose effect is to increase the number of two earner families, thereby altering the role of fathers as the sole breadwinner in those families. Perhaps more important for fathers is the fact that they work an average of 46 hours per week, with a third working 50 hours per week or more[143]. Mothers typically work an average of 15 hours per week less than fathers. Fathers are also more likely to work unsocial hours than mothers: two thirds of fathers do Saturday work, nearly half do evening work, and two fifths do Sunday work, and a quarter do night work. In general, Irish fathers and mothers seem to work longer hours outside the home than most of their EU counterparts, with the possible exception of Britain, and these work patterns clearly have a major impact on the amount of time which fathers spend in the home.

The powerful influence exercised by work in drawing parents out of the home stands in stark contrast to the growing expectations in society generally that parents – but especially fathers – should be spending more time with their children. In other words, fathers and possibly mothers too, are increasingly expected to give more time both at home and at work. These developments place parents in an awkward psychological position because, in family matters, financial investment without emotional involvement no longer caries the esteem that it once did.

There is a growing recognition in policy circles that family-friendly measures are needed – such as flexible working (job-sharing, flexitime, working from home, part-time working, etc.), leave arrangements (maternity leave, paternity leave, adoption leave, etc.), breaks (employment breaks, sabbaticals, secondments, etc.), and other initiatives (such as childcare support, employee assistance programmes, etc)[144] - so that parents can become more involved in the care of their children while at the same time being more available for work. However the research suggests that fathers - and men generally - are less likely to avail of family-friendly measures than women and mothers because of factors such as loss of earnings which can have a negative effect on the entire family, increased workload resulting from taking time off and the fear that taking leave for family reasons may have a negative impact on one's career[145]. In addition, the culture of the workplace may discourage men from availing of family friendly measures because it does not expect men who are fathers to behave any differently to men who are not fathers. In addition, most of the arguments in favour of family-friendly measures in the workplace are advanced from the perspective of

[143] See McKeown, Ferguson and Rooney, 1998, Chapter Five for more detailed statistics.
[144] See Humphreys, Fleming and O'Donnell, 2000.
[145] Fynes, Morrissey, Roche, Whelan and Williams, 1996. It is significant that three quarters of all part-time work in Ireland in 2000 was undertaken by women although this should be seen in the context that only 17% of all employment is part-time so that, in general, women, like men, are much more likely to be in full-time than part-time employment (Quarterly National Household Survey, 2000).

women's equality in the labour market rather than from the perspective of men and fathers[146]. It also needs to be emphasised that family friendly measures, as the term is normally used, do not cover the number of hours worked by fathers even though this is one of the more important factors determining these fathers' involvement with children.

3. How are men initiated into fatherhood?

It is hard to state precisely where the process of becoming a father begins: at the moment of the child's conception? at the birth of the child? or when the baby is first planned? The vagueness of the father's relationship to the child - and of his rights to the child while in the womb - mirrors the vagueness of the father's role in general and is probably independent of the father's marital or residential status.

By comparison with the process of becoming a mother - which is clearly signalled in the woman's pregnancy and the physical changes in her body over nine months before giving birth - the process of becoming a father normally has no outward signs for a man. Pregnancy therefore is the period when women prepare and - through ante-natal visits and classes as well as reading books and leaflets - are prepared for motherhood. Moreover, while men cannot get pregnant, it has been assumed, at least until recently, that men do not need to be involved in the ante-natal process of preparing for fatherhood. Even books on pregnancy, childbirth and child rearing tend to directed at women rather than men. As one researcher has pointed out: "structural disincentives for male involvement in pregnancy are legion"[147].

These considerations suggest that some of the existing conventions surrounding pregnancy, childbirth and child rearing may need re-examination if men are to identify more fully with the fatherhood role. It might be asked, for example, if ante-natal classes are sufficiently inclusive of and sympathetic to men? Does the information provided through text, pictures, and videos portray a full and positive role for fathers? Is it appropriate that there is no paternity leave for fathers which would facilitate bonding with their new-born child just as there is maternity leave for mothers in recognition of the physical demands of childbearing and breast-feeding? Much of the research evidence suggests that, with better preparation for fatherhood and parenthood, the attachment between father and child - as well as between father and mother - can be greatly strengthened; in addition, fathers become more involved with the child after its birth[148].

4. What impact do fathers have on children?

The well-being of children is influenced by two key factors[149]: (1) economic or material well-being and (2) relational well-being, the latter referring to the quality of both parent-parent relationships and parent-child relationships. Fathers, like mothers, have a crucial influence on both these aspects of well-being.

[146]Second Commission on the Status of Women, 1993; Employment Equality Agency, 1996; Commission on the Family, 1998; National Economic and Social Council, 1996; 1999; Partnership 2000 Expert Working Group on Childcare, 1999.
[147]Burgess, 1997:112-113
[148]Jackson, 1984; Nickel and Kocher, 1987; Cowan, 1988; Brazelton and Cramer, 1991
[149]Amato, 1993; Amato and Keith, 1991; Amato, Loomis and Booth, 1995; Cooksey, 1997; Downey, 1994; Goodman, Emery and Haugaard, 1998; Hetherington and Stanley-Hagan, 1997; Hines, 1997; McLanahan, 1997; McLanahan and Sandefur, 1994; McLanahan and Teitler, 1999; Najman, Behrens, Andersen, Bor, O'Callaghan, and Williams, 1997; Seltzer, 1994; Thomson, Hanson and McLanahan, 1994

As regards the material well-being of children, one of the most consistent findings to emerge from research is that educational outcomes (such as completion of second and third level education) are heavily influenced by the income level of parents, particularly the income of parents when the child is under the age of five[150]. Given that the presence of fathers tends to improve the material well-being of households, it follows that fathers will also tend to have beneficial educational outcomes for children. This conclusion is consistent with other studies which suggest that "the contribution of resources, both economic and psychological, from fathers may be the key contributing factor in the educational achievement of young adults"[151].

As regards the relational well-being of children, a key finding to emerge from extensive research is that children are adversely affected by conflict and instability within the family. According to one review of 12 different US studies: "family structure is more important than poverty in determining behavioural and psychological problems"[152]. Other studies and reviews have reached similar conclusions[153]. These studies do not allow one to separate the influence of fathers from the rest of the family system although they clearly show that fathers are important to the well-being of children. For example, the adverse consequences of separation and divorce on children, even in low conflict situations, cannot be unrelated to the absence of fathers in the lives of children given that, in most cases, they result in the father leaving home. Similarly the benign effects of stable, conflict-free, two parent families must also reflect the benign effects which fathers, no less than mothers, have on the well-being of children. One review summarised the implications of this research as follows: "In sum, research suggests that if we are concerned about optimising children's health and development, we should be promoting and supporting both two-parent family structure plus ways to involve fathers in their children's lives – whatever the family form"[154].

A particularly interesting finding from research on the relational well-being of families is the way in which parent-parent relationships emerge as central to the well-being of children[155]. This suggests that services to promote the well-being of children need to focus not just on material well-being but also on relational well-being through parent-child as well as parent-parent relationships.

5. How does the law treat fathers?

The Irish Constitution makes no explicit reference to fathers, married or otherwise. Mothers are explicitly mentioned - if not to the delight of all women - in the context of their contribution to the common good by working at home (Article 41.2.1) and the need to ensure that they do not neglect their home duties by having to engage in outside work (Article 41.2.2).

Within the Irish Constitution, the family is based on marriage and, as such, unmarried fathers are not part of a family and therefore have no constitutional rights to children born outside of marriage. Within European

---

[150]Duncan & Brooks-Gunn, 1997; see also Cameron, & Heckman, 1999; McLanahan, 1997.
[151]Furstenberg, 1990:155.
[152]McLanahan, 1997.
[153]Najman, Behrens, Andersen, Bor, O'Callaghan, and Williams, 1997; Wilkinson, 1996:166; Booth, 1999:40.
[154]Levine and Pitt, 1995:25.
[155]Lamb, 1997.

Law however, the European Convention on Human Rights confers a "right to respect for family life" (Article 8) which is not confined solely to marriage-based relationships but may encompass other de facto family ties where the parties are living together outside marriage. According to the European Court: "A child born out of such a relationship is ipso iure part of that "family" unit from the moment of his birth and by the very fact of it. There thus exists between the child and his parents a bond amounting to family life even if at the time of his or her birth the parents are no longer cohabiting or if their relationship has then ended"[156].

The situation in Ireland regarding the rights of unmarried fathers and their children is contrary to the UN Declaration on the Rights of the Child, Article 7, Paragraph 1 of which states: "The child shall be registered immediately after birth and shall have the right from birth to a name, the right to acquire a nationality and, as far as possible, the right to know and be cared for by his or her parents". Commenting on this situation, the UN Committee on the Rights of the Child – whose function is to oversee implementation of the UN Declaration on the Rights of the Child in Ireland and elsewhere - has expressed its concern about "the disadvantaged situation of children born of unmarried parents due to the lack of appropriate procedures to name the father in the birth registration of the child"[157].

The reality of life for single fathers – as indeed for single mothers - is that most of them live in relatively disadvantaged circumstances; most of them have low levels of education and poor earning capacity; many of them are not able to meet the cost of independently supporting a family. Without the intervention of the State, family life in these disadvantaged communities would be virtually impossible. However the particular way in which the State intervenes to help lone mothers and fathers through the One-parent Family Payment – and the ideologies which support this intervention - is such as to add to the social exclusion of lone fathers by effectively prohibiting cohabiting and co-parenting[158]. As a result, many lone fathers not only face exclusion from the labour market and an important source of identity and fulfilment through work, but they also face the even deeper social exclusion from family life and an irreplaceable stakeholding in society through parenting their children as breadwinners and homemakers. Many children in these families also suffer from not having a father living with them or even in regular contact with them.

6. How do non-resident fathers parent their children?

The term "non-resident" father is used to denote the reality of those fathers who, for whatever reason, do not live with their children. Fathers in such circumstances typically experience more difficulty in being actively involved in parenting their children compared to resident fathers. Research on non-resident fathers has tended to focus on two aspects of the parenting relationship: the frequency of contact and the payment of maintenance.

Contrary to popular belief, research in Ireland[159] and Britain[160], reveals that a majority of non-resident fathers stay in contact with their children. Two

---

[156]European Court of Human Rights, 1994:3.
[157]United Nations Committee on the Rights of the Child, 1998, paragraph 17, p.7; see also The Children's Right's Alliance, 1997, paragraphs 99-101, p.23.
[158]See McKeown, 2001.
[159]Richardson and Kernan, 1992:83
[160]Bradshaw, Stimson, Skinner and Williams, 1999a.

sets of factors are important in determining the level of contact. The first is having a good relationship with the mother and the second is the father's socio-economic characteristics such as being in employment, living close, having only one child, and living in a household without children.

The payment of maintenance by non-resident fathers seems to vary considerably from one country to another. In Ireland, the proportion of one parent households in receipt of maintenance from non-resident fathers, where the household is also in receipt of the One-Parent Family Payment, is about 20% in the case of single parents and 30% in the case of separated and divorced parents[161]. In the UK, the corresponding figure is around 30% of one parent households[162]. Studies in the US suggest much higher level of payment with 67% of single non-resident fathers paying at least some maintenance compared to 84% in the case of divorced non-resident fathers[163].

A fundamental issue affecting the payment of maintenance is the perceived legitimacy of the arrangement, particularly in the highly charged context where non-resident fathers are expected to pay maintenance while access to the children may be restricted by the mother. The importance of maintenance arrangements which are legitimised in the context of joint parenting was also underlined by the Commission on the Family: "The Commission considers that realising the potential of improving income for lone parents through adequate maintenance arrangements for children, has to be part of a longer-term strategy involving the promotion of responsible joint parenting by young women and men which is desirable in their child's interest"[164]. In addition to issues of legitimacy, there are often very practical considerations which affect the payment of maintenance such as the father's ability to pay as measured by income and employment status.

7. How do step-fathers parent their children?

The term "stepfamily" refers to families which are created when a parent takes a new partner, whether through marriage or cohabitation[165]. The number of stepfamilies is on the increase and is part and parcel of the growing process of breakdown and reconstitution among families. A crucial question in the present context concerns the impact which stepfathers have on the well-being of children. One of the obvious benefits of stepfathers is that they normally increase household income which improves the children's standard of living[166]. Paradoxically, the entry of a stepfather can also have the effect of diminishing the role of non-resident biological fathers.

---

[161] See Department of Social, Community and Family Affairs, 2000:107-108

[162] Bradshaw and Millar, 1991

[163] Meyer, 1999:139-140

[164] Commission on the Family, 1998:115. Some of the difficulties which arise in this regard in Ireland are illustrated dramatically in a recent study which found that young single mothers would prefer not to accept maintenance since "if the father paid maintenance this would undermine their ability to control access and to protect their children(as they saw it)" (Russell and Corcoran, 2000:17). These mothers would prefer the State to deduct maintenance straight from earnings or benefits "as a way of ensuring the payment was more regular and of avoiding contact with an ex-partner" (ibid:18). Perhaps even more discouraging is the fact that the study erroneously interprets these findings as providing "support for the DSCFA taking a more active role in pursuing the absent parent for maintenance and for collecting such payments" (ibid:19). Such an interpretation is quite at variance with the views of the Commission on the Family and, if the experience of the Child Support Agency in Britain is any guide, would further damage relationships in these fragile families. It is not without good reason that social policy analysts have described the Child Support Agency in Britain as "the worst policy-making disaster in modern British history" (Bradshaw, Stimson, Skinner and Williams, 1999b:416).

[165] Bornat, Dimmock, Jones and Peace, 1999:251.

[166] Teachman and Paasch, 1994.

Despite improvements in material well-being associated with stepfathers, the research suggests that other forms of child well-being, notably psychological and behavioural adjustment, are not improved by the presence of a stepparent, either stepfather or stepmother[167]. The main reason why stepfamilies do not improve the well-being of children – which may already have been impaired by previous experiences of family life – seems to be due to the fact that relations between stepparents and stepchildren are not always close or even friendly. Despite this, there is also evidence that when relations between stepparents and stepchildren are close, children appear to benefit. Extended stepfamilies are sources of support but they tend to be less so than traditional kin networks of never-divorced parents.

Overall, the evidence on stepfathers, and stepfamilies generally, suggests that they are likely to be more vulnerable than conventional two parent families, particularly in terms of relational well-being and its associated outcomes. Some of these vulnerabilities, particularly in the case of children, arise as much from the breakdown of their first family as from the reconstitution of their second[168]. In Ireland, as elsewhere, the needs of these families require careful and sensitive consideration and new policies and practices may have to be devised to promote their well-being.

8. How can family services support fathers?

The predominant focus of services for families is on mothers rather than fathers. There is a good deal of research and practice to suggest that fathers tend to be avoided by professionals – and possibly vice versa – and there is great uncertainty among professionals about how to approach fathers and work with them[169] In social work as in family support, parenting is often treated as synonymous with mothering and tends to "filter out fathers"[170].

There is now a growing recognition that services need to be developed to support fathers as part of a broader strategy of promoting the well-being of children and families, including the well-being of men and women. The development of services for fathers faces a number of specific challenges including:

- Finding out the needs of fathers, particularly the needs of different types of vulnerable fathers, and the most appropriate types of service response; it is worth reflecting that the low uptake of existing services by fathers may itself be an indication that many of these services are inappropriate.
- Adopting and promoting a strengths-based perspective to work with fathers as with families generally; too often, it would appear, fathers are seen by professionals from a negative "deficit perspective" rather than as persons with needs, strengths and capabilities.
- Training professionals to see fathers as part of the family even where they are not living in the same household as the mother and child; it is no longer valid to assume that the household and the family are the same thing given the extent of marital breakdown and of births outside marriage.
- Recruiting more men into the caring professions so that services to families are seen as the business of men as much as women; this does not imply that only men can only work with men but it does suggest that

---

[167] Amato, 1999:169.
[168] Harold, Pryor and Reynolds, 2001:5.
[169] See, Roberts and Macdonald, 1999:63; French, 1998:187-188; see also Rylands, 1995; Murphy, 1996:95; Bernard Van Leer Foundation, 2001:3.
[170] Buckley, 1998.

the work of caring, both inside and outside the family, is an appropriate calling for both men and women and this is not reflected in the current gender-imbalance in the caring professions.

- Promoting awareness of family services in a way which is seen as supportive of men and fathers at every stage of the life cycle from child birth to old age; many of the existing images of family services focus primarily on the mother and child.

The practicalities of making family services more inclusive of fathers is a major challenge. Research on best practice in this area suggests that two key stages are involved[171]. The first involves an audit of existing attitudes among management, staff and parents within the service to the involvement of fathers while the second stage involves developing a concrete strategy for father involvement.

9. Can fathering skills be taught?

Parenting, whether by mothers or fathers, is much more than a skill. It is a way of being a person and of being in relationship. This is worth affirming in view of the tendency to see parenting problems as essentially as "skill deficits" which can be rectified by imparting techniques. Techniques may indeed help but only if they help parents to develop as persons and to form healthy parent-child as well as parent-parent relationships.

The way in which men play the role of father inevitably varies widely according to their own experiences of being men and of being fathered, their marital and residential status, the number and ages of their children, their social class and employment status, and the relative importance which they attribute - consciously or unconsciously - to work and to fathering and to seeing fathering as valuable work. Inevitably, in view of such complexity, there are many ways to be a good father just as there are many ways to be a good mother. Parenting skills need to build on this diversity and respect it rather than try to erase it.

In trying to define what is a "good enough" father, I have come to the somewhat minimalist conclusion that the good enough father must have a strong but flexible bond of attachment through which the child feels safe and protected. This bond should allow for both closeness and distance as other commentators have observed: "A father who is too close or too remote will not be good enough. ... In contrast, the good father is able to successfully maintain the golden mean. Such a father is close but not too close, strong but not overwhelming, loving but not seductive, supportive but able to discipline, caring but encouraging autonomy"[172]. Needless to say, a good mother will also have these attributes.

---

[171] See Levine, Murphy, and Wilson, 1998; Levine and Pitt, 1995; Burgess and Ruxton, 1996.

Concluding Comment

A key theme which informs this report is that no one should be left out of the family picture. An inclusive society requires an inclusive family. Mothers, fathers and children, including the extended family, are all part of the family picture which, for all the vicissitudes of family life, is part of the reality to which everyone belongs; family histories are dotted by the abiding presences of absent members. At various times in history, ways of thinking about the family have tended to displace, distort or simply ignore the lived experiences of different family members be they mothers, children or fathers and, inevitably, new ways of thinking about families have always emerged to redirect attention towards these blind spots. This report is part of a process of keeping fathers in the family picture alongside mothers and children and, as such, is based on the belief that an inclusive family helps to create an inclusive society.

Bibliography

Abramovitch, H., 1997. "Images of the 'Father' in Psychology and Religion", in Lamb, M., (Editor), The Role of the Father in Child Development, Third Edition, New York: John Wiley and Sons, pp. 19-32.

Amato, PR., 1993. "Children's Adjustment to Divorce: Theories, Hypotheses and Empirical Support", Journal of Marriage and the Family, 55, 23-38.

Amato, PR., 1994a. "Father-child Relations, Mother-child Relations, and Offspring Psychological Well-being in Early Adulthood", Journal of Marriage and the Family, 56, pp.1031-1042.

Amato, PR., 1994b. "The Implications of Research Findings on Children in Stepfamilies", in Booth, A., and Dunn, J., (Editors), Stepfamilies: Who Benefits? Who Does Not?, Hillsdale NJ: Lawrence Erlbaum, pp.55-79.

Amato, PR., and Booth, A., 1997. A Generation at Risk: Growing Up in an Era of Family Upheaval, Harvard: Harvard University Press.

Amato, PR., and Gilbreth, JG., 2000. "Non-Resident Fathers and Children's Well-Being: A Meta-Analysis", Journal of Marriage and the Family, 62.

Amato, PR., and Keith, B., 1991. "Parental Divorce and the Well-Being of Children: A Meta-Analysis", Psychological Bulletin, 110, 26-46.55.

Amato, PR., Loomis, LS., and Booth, A., 1995. "Parental Divorce, Marital Conflict and Offspring Well-Being During Early Adulthood", Social Forces, 73, 896-916.

Anderson, R., 1999. Warm Smiles from Cold Mountains: Dharma Talks on Zen Meditation, Berkeley, California: Rodmell Press.

Andrews, P., 1994. Changing Children: Living with a New Generation, Dublin: Gill and Macmillian.

Andrews, P., 2000. "Concerns and Hopes" in A Book of Letters: Hopes and Aspirations for the Children of the Next Millennium, London: The Lillie Road Centre Group of Homes.

Annuarium Statisticum Ecclesiae, 1987 and 1997. Statistical Yearbook of the Church, 1987 and 1999. Civitas Vaticana: Typic Polyglottis Varticanis.

Barrett, Callan, Doris, O'Neill, Russell, Sweetman and McBride, 2000. How Unequal? Men and Women in the Irish Labour Market, Dublin: Oak Tree Press in association with the Economic and Social Research Institute.

Bernard Van Leer Foundation, 2001. Early Childhood Matters: The Bulletin of the Bernard Van Leer Foundation, No 97, February, The Hague, Netherlands: Bernard Van Leer Foundation. www.bernardvanleer.org

Bogenschneider, K., 1997. "Parental Involvement in Adolescent Schooling: A Proximal Process with Transcontextual Validity", Journal of Marriage and the Family, 59, pp.718-734.

Booth, A., 1999. "Causes and Consequences of Divorce: Reflections on Recent Research", in Thompson, RA., and Amato, PR., (Editors), The Postdivorce Family: Children, Parenting and Society, London: Sage Publications, pp.29-48.

Bornat, J., Dimmnock, B., Jones, D., and Peace, S., 1999. "The Impact of Family Change on Older People: The Case of Stepfamilies" in McRae, S., (Editor), Changing Britain: Families and Households in the 1990s, Oxford: Oxford University Press, pp.248-262.

Bradshaw, J., and Millar, J., 1991. Lone Parent Families in the UK, Department of Social Security Research Report Number 6, London: HMSO.

Bradshaw, J., Stimson, C., Skinner, C., and Williams, J., 1999a. Absent Fathers?, London: Routledge.

Bradshaw, J., Stimson, C., Skinner, C., and Williams, J., 1999b. "Non-Resident Fathers in Britain", in McRae, S., (Editor), Changing Britain: Families and Households in the 1990s, pp.404-426, Oxford: Oxford University Press.

Brannen, J., Moss, P., Owen, C., and Wale, C., 1997. Mothers, Fathers and Employment: Parents and the Labour Market in Britain 1984-1994, Research Report Number 10, London: Department for Education and Employment.

Brazelton, TB., and Cramer, BG., 1991. The Earliest Relationship, London: Karnac.

Breen, R., Hannan, DF., Rottman, DB., and Whelan, CT., 1990. Understanding Contemporary Ireland: State, Class and Development in the Republic of Ireland, Dublin: Gill and Macmillian.

Buchanan, CM., Maccoby, EE., and Dornbusch, SM., 1996. Adolescents After Divorce, Cambridge MA: Harvard University Press.

Buckley, H., 1998. "Filtering Out Fathers: The Gendered Nature of Social Work in Child Protection", Irish Social Worker, Volume 16, Number 3, pp.7-11.

Bumpass, L., and Hsien-Hen Lu., 2000. "Cohabitation: How the Families of US Children are Changing", Focus, Volume 21, Number 1, Spring, pp.5-8. Published by the Institute for Research on Poverty at the University of Wisconsin-Madison.

Burgess, A., 1997. Fatherhood Reclaimed: The Making of the Modern Father, London: Vermillion.

Burgess, A., and Ruxton, S., 1996. Men and Their Children: Proposals for Public Policy, London: Institute for Public Policy Research.

Burghes, L., Clarke, L., and Cronin, N., 1997. Fathers and Fatherhood in Britain, Occasional Paper 23, July, London: Family Policy Studies Centre.

Burtless, G., 1999. "Effects of Growing Wage Disparities and Changing Family Composition on the U.S. Income Distribution", CSED Working Paper No. 4, July. Washington, D. C The Brookings Institution.

Cameron, S., & Heckman, J. J., 1999. "Can Tuition Policy Combat Rising Wage Inequality?" in Kosters, M., ed., Financing College Tuition: Government Policies, Social Priorities. Washington, D.C.: AEI Press.

Cantillon, S. and Nolan, B., 1998. "Are Married Women More Deprived than their Husbands?", Journal of Social Policy, Volume 27(2), pp.151-171.

Carlsen, S., 1993. "New Scandinavian Experiences" in Fathers in Families of Tomorrow, Report from the Conference held in Copenhagen, 17-18 June 1993, Copenhagen: The Ministry of Social Affairs.

Carroll, S., 2000. Things for Dads to Do with Kids, Dublin: Parental Equality Publishing.

Clare, A., 2000. On Men: Masculinity in Crisis, London: Chatto & Windus.

Coleman, DA., 1999. "Demography and Migration in Ireland, North and South", in Heath, AF., Breen, R., and Whelan, CT., (Editors), Ireland North and South: Perspectives from Social Science, Proceedings of the British Academy, Volume 98, pp. 69-115, Oxford: Oxford University Press.

Colman, A., and Colman, L., 1988. The Father: Mythology and Changing Roles, Illinois: Chiron Publications.

Commission on the Family, 1996. Strengthening Families for Life, Interim Report, November, Dublin: Stationery Office.

Commission on the Family, 1998. Strengthening Families for Life, Main Report, July, Dublin: Stationery Office.

Cooksey, EC., 1997. "Consequences of Young Mothers' Marital Histories for Children's Cognitive Development", Journal of Marriage and the Family, 59, 245-261.

Council of Europe, 1995. "Ireland", in Conference of European Ministers Responsible for Family Affairs, Twenty Fourth Session, Helsinki, Finland, 26-28 June, Strasbourg: Council of Europe.

Cousins, M., 1997. A Review of the Department of Social, Community and Family Affairs' Scheme of Grants for Locally Based Men's Groups, October, Dublin: Department of Social, Community and Family Affairs.

Cowan, CP. and PA., 1988a. Men's Involvement in Parenthood: Identifying the Antecedents and Understanding the Barriers", in Berman, PW., and Pederson, FA., (Editors), Men's Transitions to Fatherhood: Longitudinal Studies in Early Family Experience, New Jersey: Lawrence Erlbaum.

Cowan, CP. and PA., 1988b. "Working with Men Becoming Fathers: The Impact of a Couples Group Intervention", in Bronstein P., and Cowan C. and P. (Editors), Fatherhood Today, New York: John Wiley and Sons.

Department of Enterprise and Employment, 1993. Economic Status of School-Leavers 1991, Dublin: Department of Enterprise and Employment.

Department of Education and Science, 2000. Exploring Masculinities: A Programme in Personal and Social Development for Transition Year and Senior Cycle Boys and Young Men, Dublin: Department of Education and Science.

Department of Labour, 1991. Economic Status of School-Leavers 1990, Dublin: Department of Labour.

Department of Social, Community and Family Affairs, 2000. Review of the One-Parent Family Payment, Programme Evaluation Report No 7, September, Dublin: Stationery Office.

Dooley, D., 1998. "Gendered Citizenship in the Irish Constitution", in Murphy, T., and Twomey, P., (Editors), Ireland's Evolving Constitution, 1937-1997: Collected Essays, Oxford: Hart Publishing, pp.121-134.

Downey, DB., 1994. "The School Performance of Children from Single-Mother and Single-Father Families: Economic or Interpersonal Deprivation", Journal of Family Issues, 15, 129-147.

Dromey, M., and Doherty, M., 1992. "Fathers' Involvement with their Non-Marital Children", Paper delivered to Conference on Surviving Childhood Adversity, Trinity College Dublin.

Duncan, G. J., & Brooks–Gunn, J., 1997. "Income Effects Across the Life Span: Integration and Interpretation", in Duncan, G. J., & Brooks-Gunn, J., eds., Consequences of Growing Up Poor. New York: Russell Sage Foundation.

Employment Equality Agency, 1996. Introducing Family–Friendly Initiatives in the Workplace, Researched and written by Hugh Fisher, Dublin: Employment Equality Agency.

Emery, R., 1999. "Postdivorce Family Life for Children: An Overview of Research and Some Implications for Policy" in Thompson, RA., and Amato, PR., (Editors), The Postdivorce Family: Children, Parenting and Society, London: Sage Publications, pp.3-27.

Eurobarometer 39.0, 1993. Europeans and the Family: Results of an Opinion Survey, December, Brussels: Commission of the European Communities, Directorate General V for Employment, Industrial Relations and Social Affairs.

European Commission Network on Childcare, 1990. Men as Carers for Children, Brussels: European Commission Network on Childcare.

European Commission Network on Childcare, 1993. Men as Carers: Report of an International Seminar in Ravenna, Italy, 21-22 May, Brussels: European Commission Network on Childcare.

European Court of Human Rights, 1994. "Judgement in the Case of Keegan v. Ireland", Strasbourg: European Court of Human Rights.

Fahey, T., Fitz Gerald, J., and Maitre, B., 1998. "The Economic and Social Implications of Demographic Change", Journal of the Statistical and Social Inquiry Society of Ireland, Volume 27, Part 5, pp. 185-222.

Fahey, T., and Lyons, M., 1995. Marital Breakdown and Family Law in Ireland, Oak Tree Press in association with The Economic and Social Research Institute.

Farrell, W., 2001. Father and Child Reunion: How to Bring the Dads We Need to the Children We Love, New York: Penguin Putnam.

Farrington, D., P., and Hawkin, J.D. "Predicting Participation, Early Onset and Later Persistence in Officially Recorded Offending" in Criminal Behaviour and Mental Health, Volume 1, pp. 1-33.

Fathers Direct, 1999. The Bounty Guide to Fatherhood, London: Fathers Direct.

Featherstone, B., and Holloway, W., (Editors), 1997. Motherhood and Ambivalence, London: Routledge.

Ferri, E., and Smith, K., 1995. Parenting in the 1990s. London: Family Policy Study Centre.

Flanagan, N., and Richardson, V., 1992. Unmarried Mothers: A Social Profile, Dublin: Department of Social Policy and Social Work, University College Dublin.

Flanagan, N., 2001. "Born Outside Marriage: The Social Implications for Irish Pre-School Children", in Cleary, A., Nic Giolla Phadraig, M., and Quin, S., (Editors), Understanding Children - Volume Two: Changing Experiences and Family Forms, Dublin: Oak Tree Press, Chapter Two, pp.19-45.

Flynn, L.,1998. "To be an Irish Man – Constructions of Masculinity within the Constitution", in Murphy, T., and Twomey, P., (Editors), Ireland's Evolving Constitution, 1937-1997: Collected Essays, Oxford: Hart Publishing, pp.135-146.

French, G., 1998. Enhancing Our Future: A Profile of Parenting Programmes in Ireland, Dublin: Barnardos and the Department of Health&Children.

Freud, S., 1954. The Interpretation of Dreams, Standard Edition, Volumes 3,4, Hogarth Press.: London.

Freud, S., 1966. Standard Edition of the Complete Psychological Works of Sigmund Freud , The Hogarth Press and the Institute of Psychoanalysis: London.

Freud, S., 1977. On Sexuality, Vol. 7, Penguin Books.

Freud, S., 1984. 'A Note on the Unconscious in Psychoanalysis' (1912), P.F.L. Vol. 11, London: Pelican Books.

Furstenberg, FF., 1990. "Coming of Age in a Changing Family System", in Feldman, SS., and Elliott, GR., (Editors), At the Threshold: The Developing Adolescent, Cambridge MA: Harvard University Press.

Furstenberg, F., and Cherlin, A., 1991. Divided Families: What Happens to Children When Parents Part, Cambridge MA: Harvard University Press.

Fynes, B., Morrissey, T., Roche, W., Whelan, B., and Williams, J., 1996. Flexible Working Lives: The Changing Nature of Working Time Arrangements in Ireland, Dublin: Oak Tree Press in association with Graduate School of Business, University College Dublin.

Gallagher, C., !986. The Function of the Father in the Family: Psychoanalytic Notes. Studies (Summer).

Gardner, LP., 1943. "A Survey of the Attitudes and Activities of Fathers", Journal of Genetic Psychology, 63, 15-53.

Garfinkel, I., and Klawitter, MM., 1990. "The Effect of Routine Income Withholding of Child Support Collections", Journal of Policy Analysis and Management, 9, 155-177.

Gbrich, C., 1987, "Primary Caregiver Fathers: A Role Study, Some Preliminary Findings", Australian Journal of Sex, Marriage and Family, Volume 8, Number 2.

Ghate, D., Shaw, C., and Hazel, N., 2000. Fathers and Family Centres: Engaging Fathers in Preventative Services, Joseph Rowntree Foundation – Findings, York: York Publishing Services. www.jrf.org.uk

Goodman, GS., Emery, RE., and Haugaard, JJ., 1998. "Developmental Psychology and Law: The Cases of Divorce, Child Maltreatment, Foster Care and Adoption", in Damon, W., Sigel, I., and Renninger, A., (Editors), Handbook of Child Psychology, Fifth Edition, Volume 4, Child Psychology in Practice, pp.775-874, New York: Wiley.

Gorrel Barnes, G., Thompson, P., Daniel, G., and Burchardt, N., 1998. Growing Up in Stepfamilies, Oxford: Oxford University Press.

Government of Ireland, 1996. Partnership 2000 for Inclusion, Employment and Competitiveness, Dublin: The Stationery Office.

Government of Ireland, 1999. National Development Plan 2000-2006, November, Dublin: The Stationery Office.

Government of Ireland, 2000. Programme for Prosperity and Fairness, February, Dublin: The Stationery Office.

Harold, G., Pryor, J., and Reynolds, J., 2001. Not in Front of the Children? How Conflict Between Parents Affects Children, London: One Plus One Marriage and Partnership Research.

Hawkins, A., Christiansen, S.L., Pond Sargent, K. and Hill, E.J., 1995. "Rethinking Fathers Involvement in Child Care: A Developmental Perspective". In W. Marsiglio, (Editor), Fatherhood: Contemporary Theory, Research, and Social Policy, London: Sage.

Hetherington, EM., and Clingempeel, WG., 1992. Coping with Marital Transitions, Monographs of the Society for Research in Child Development, Volume 57, Number 2-3, Chicago IL: University of Chicago Press.

Hetherington, EM., and Jodl, KM., 1994. "Stepfamilies as Settings for Child Development", in Booth, A., and Dunn, J., (Editors), Stepfamilies: Who Benefits? Who Does Not?, Hillsdale NJ: Lawrence Erlbaum, pp.55-79.

Hetherington, EM., and Stanley–Haagen, MM., 1997. "The Effects of Divorce on Fathers and Their Children" in Lamb, ME., (Editor), The Role of the Father in Child Development, Third Edition, pp.191-211, New York: Wiley.

Hillman, J., 1994. We've Had a Hundred Years of Psychotherapy and the World's Getting Worse, New York: Random House.

Hillman, J., 1996. The Soul's Code: In Search of Character and Calling, New York: Random House.

Hines, AM., 1997. "Divorce-Related Transitions, Adolescent Development and the Role of the Parent-Child Relationship: A Review of the Literature", Journal of Marriage and the Family, 59, 375-388.

Humphreys, PC., Fleming, S., and O'Donnell, O., 2000. Balancing Work and Family Life: The Role of Flexible Working Arrangements, Dublin: Institute of Public Administration.

Ireland, 1999. National Development Plan 2000-2006, November, Dublin: Stationery Office.

Jackson, B., 1984. Fatherhood, London: Allen and Unwin.

Jones, S., 1998. Supporting Ireland's Children: An Independent Evaluation of Barnardos's Family Support Project, Moyross, Limerick, Dublin: Barnardos.

Jung, ., 1925. "Marriage as a Psychological Relationship", in Collected Works, Volume 17, London: Routledge and Kegan Paul, pp. 189-201.

Jung, C., 1994. Quoted in Ellenberger, H., The Discovery of the Unconscious: The History and Evolution of Dynamic Psychiatry, London: Fontana Press. Jung's quotation was first published in 1942.

Kane, S., 2001. An Exploration of the Perceptions and Experiences of Non-Resident Fathers, M.Sc. Thesis in Child Protection and Welfare at the Department of Social Studies, Trinity College Dublin.

Kaufman, FX., Kuijsten, A., Schulze, HJ., and Strohmeier, KP., 1997. Family Life and Family Policies in Europe, Volume One: Structures and Trends in the 1980s, Oxford: Clarendon Press.

Keen, S., 1991. Fire in the Belly: On Being a Man, New York: Bantam Books.

Kiely, G., 1995. "Fathers in Families". In I., Colgan McCarthy, (Editor), Irish Family Studies: Selected Papers, University College Dublin, pp. 147-158.

Kraemer, S., 1995. "Parenting Yesterday, Today and Tomorrow", in Utting, D., (Editor), Families and Parenting Conference Report: Proceedings of a Conference held in London, 26 September 1995, London: Family Policy Studies Centre.

Kwong, MI., Bartholomew, K., and Dutton, DG., 1999. "Gender Differences in Patterns of Relationship Violence in Alberta", Canadian Journal of Behavioural Science, 31:3, pp.150-160.

Labour Force Survey, 1996. Dublin: Stationery Office.

Lacan, J.,1951. "Intervention on Transference", in Mitchell, J., and Rose, J., (Editors) 1982, Feminine Sexuality, London: Macmillan.

Lacan, J., 1953. The Neurotics Individual Myth, Psych Quat, 1979 Trs. Evans.

Lacan, J., 1958. The Family, Unpublished , Translated by Cormac Gallagher.

Lacan, J., 1973. The Four Fundamental Concepts (Le Seminaire de Jacques Lacan, Paris) 1979, London: Penguin.

Lacan, J., 1977. Ecrits: A selection, Tavistock, Routledge.

Lamb, M., 1997. "Fathers and Child Development: An Introductory Overview and Guide", in Lamb, M., (Editor), The Role of the Father in Child Development, Third Edition, New York: John Wiley and Sons, pp.1-18.

Lamb, M., 1999. "Noncustodial Fathers and Their Impact on the Children of Divorce", in Thompson, RA., and Amato, PR., (Editors), The Postdivorce Family: Children, Parenting and Society, pp.105-125, London: Sage.

Layte, R., 1999. Divided Time: Gender, Paid Employment and Domestic Labour, Aldershot UK: Ashgate.

Leonard, H, 1995. "The Stroke of a Pen", in Hyde, T., (Editor), Fathers and Sons, Dublin: Wolfhound Press, pp.36-38.

Levine, JA., Murphy, DT., and Wilson, S., 1998. New Expectations: Community Strategies for Responsible Fatherhood, New York: Families and Work Institute. www.familiesandwork.org

Levine, JA., and Pittinsky, TL., 1997. Working Fathers: New Strategies for Balancing Work and Family, New York: Harcourt Brace and Company.

Levine, JA., and Pitt, EW., 1995. Getting Men Involved: Strategies for Early Childhood Programs, New York: Families and Work Institute. www.familiesandwork.org

Lewis, C., 1986. Becoming a Father. Milton Keynes: Open University Press.

Lewis, C., 1996, "Fathers and Preschoolers" in Lamb, ME., (Editor), The Role of the Father in Child Development, Third Edition, Chichester: Wiley.

Lewis, C., 2000. A Man's Place in the Home: Fathers and Families in the UK, Joseph Rowntree Foundation – Findings, York: Joseph Rowntree Foundation. www.jrf.org.uk

Lewis, C., and Warin, J., 2001. What Good Are Dads?, www.fathersdirect.com.

Lilley, M.,1997. Becoming a Father: How to Make a Success of Your Role as a Parent, How to Books – Family Reference, Oxford Road: How To Books.

Lloyd, T., 2001. What Works With Fathers?, London: Working With Men.

Lord Chancellor's Department, 1998. Court Procedures for the Determination of Paternity and The Law on Parental Responsibility for Unmarried Fathers, Consultation Paper, March, London: Lord Chancellor's Department.

Lummis, 1982. "The Historical Dimension of Fatherhood: A Case Study 1890-1914", In Mckee L. and O'Brien, M. The Father Figure. London: Tavistock Publications

McCashin, A., 1996. Lone Mothers in Ireland: A Local Study, Dublin: Combat Poverty Agency.

McCoy, S., and Whelan, BJ., 1996. Economic Status of School-Leavers 1993-1995, Dublin: Department of Enterprise and Employment.

McCoy, S., Doyle, A., and Williams, J., 1999. Economic Status of School-Leavers 1996-1997, Dublin: Department of Enterprise and Employment.

McKeown R., and Gilligan, R., 1991. "Child Sexual Abuse in he Eastern Health Board Region of Ireland in 1988: An Analysis of 512 Confirmed Cases", The Economic and Social Review, Volume 22, Number 2, January, pp.101-134.

McKeown, K., 1997. Developing Childcare Services in Disadvantaged Areas: An Evaluation of the Pilot Childcare Initiative (1994-1995). January. Dublin: Area Development Management Limited.

McKeown, K., 1999. "Review Article on the Report of the Commission on the Family", The Economic and Social Review, Volume 30, Number 2, April, pp.203-211.

McKeown, K., 2000. Supporting Families: A Guide to What Works in Family Support Services for Vulnerable Families, October, Dublin: Stationery Office.

McKeown, K., 2001. "Families and Single Fathers in Ireland", Administration: Journal of the Institute of Public Administration, Volume 49, No 1, Spring, pp. 3-24.

McKeown, K., Fitzgerald, G., and Deehan, A., 1993. The Merchants' Quay Project: A Drugs / HIV Service in the Inner City of Dublin, 1989-1992, Dublin: Franciscan Friary, Merchants' Quay.

McKeown, K., and Fitzgerald, G., 1999. Treating Drug Addiction: An Evaluation of Addiction Response Crumlin, Dublin: Addiction Response Crumlin.

McKeown, K., Haase, T., Pratschke, J., Rock, R., and Kidd, P., 2001. Unhappy Marriages: Does Counselling Help? A Report to ACCORD, March, Dublin: ACCORD.

McKeown, K., Haase, T., Pratschke, J., 2001. Distressed Relationships: Does Counselling Help? A Report to MRCS – Marriage and Relationship Counselling Services, April, Dublin: Marriage and Relationship Counselling Services.

McKeown, K., and Sweeney, J., 2001. Family Well-being and Family Policy: Review of Research on Benefits and Costs, June, Dublin: Stationery Office.

McLanahan, SS., and Sandefur, G., 1994. Growing Up With a Single Parent: What Hurts, What Helps, Cambridge MA: Harvard University Press.

McLanahan, SS., 1997. "Parent Absence or Poverty: Which Maters More?", in Duncan, GJ., Brooks-Gunn, J., (Editors), Consequences of Growing Up Poor. New York: Russell Sage Foundation.

McLanahan, SS., and Teitler, J., 1999. "The Consequence of Father Absence", in Lamb, ME., (Editor), Parenting and Child Development in 'Non-Traditional' Families, pp.83-102, Mahwah, NJ: Erlbaum.

Mahon, E., Conlon, C., and Dillon, L., 1998. Women and Crisis Pregnancy: A Report Presented to the Department of Health and Children, Dublin: Stationery Office.

Marsiglio, W., 1995. "Fathers' Diverse Life Course Patterns and Roles". In W. Marsiglio (Editor), Fatherhood: Contemporary Theory, Research, and Social Policy, London: Sage.

Martin, F., 1998. "The Family in the Constitution – Principle and Practice", in Murphy, T., and Twomey, P., (Editors), Ireland's Evolving Constitution, 1937-1997: Collected Essays, Oxford: Hart Publishing, pp.79-98.

Meade, M., 1993. Men and the Water of Life: Initiation and the Tempering of Life, New York: HarperSanFrancisco.

Meyer, DR., 1999. "Compliance with Child Support Orders in Paternity and Divorce Cases", in Thompson, RA., and Amato, PR., (Editors), The Postdivorce Family: Children, Parenting and Society, pp.127-157, London: Sage.

Morehouse Research Institute, 1997. Turning the Corner on Father Absence in Black America: A Statement from the Morehouse Conference on African American Fathers, Atlanta: Morehouse Research Institute.

Morse, B.J., 1995. "Beyond the Conflict Tactics Scale: Assessing Gender Differences in Partner Violence", Violence and Victims, 10(4)251-272.

Murphy, M., 1996. "From Prevention to 'Family Support' and Beyond: Promoting the Welfare of Irish Children", Administration, Volume 44, Number 2, Summer, pp.73-101.

Najman, J.M., Behrens, B.C., Andersen, M., Bor, W, O'Callaghan, M. and Williams, GM., 1997. "Impact of Family Type and Family Quality on Child Behaviour Problems: A Longitudinal Study", Journal of the American Academy of Child and Adolescent Psychiatry, Volume 36(10), pp. 1357-1365.

National Economic and Social Council, 1996. Strategy into the 21st Century, Report Number 99, Dublin: National Economic and Social Council.

National Economic and Social Council, 1999. Opportunities, Challenges and Capacities for Choice, Report Number 105, Dublin: National Economic and Social Council.

Newson, J. and Newson, E., 1963. Infant Care in an Urban Community. London. Allen and Unwin.

Nichols-Casebolt, A., Danziger, SK., 1989. "The Effect of Childbearing Age on Child Support Awards and Economic Well-Being Among Divorcing Mothers", Journal of Divorce, 12(4), 34-38.

Nickel H., and Kocher, N., 1987. "West Germany and German Speaking Countries" in Lamb, ME, The Father's Role: Cross Cultural Comparisons, Hillsdale NJ: Lawrence Erlbaum.

Nolan, B., O'Connell, P., and Whelan, CT., (Editors), 2000. Bust to Boom? The Irish Experience of Growth and Inequality, Dublin: Institute of Public Administration and the Economic and Social Research Institute.

Nolan, B., and Watson, D., 1999. Women and Poverty in Ireland, Dublin: Combat Poverty Agency.

O'Donohoe, G., 2001. "Parental Responses – Children's Responses", in Cleary, A., Nic Giolla Phadraig, M., and Quin, S., (Editors), Understanding Children - Volume Two: Changing Experiences and Family Forms, Dublin: Oak Tree Press, Chapter Three, pp.49-68.

O'Grady, T., 1992. "Married to the State: A Study of Unmarried Mother's Allowance Applicants", Seminar Paper presented to the Federation of Services to Unmarried Parents and their Children, December, Dublin.

O'Leary, K.D. and Arias, I., 1988. "Assessing Agreement of Reports of Spouse Abuse". In G.T. Hotaling, D. Finkelhor, J.T. Kirkpatrick and M.A. Straus (Editors.), Family Abuse and Its Consequences, London: Sage Publications.

O'Mahony, P., 1997. Mountjoy Prisoners: A Sociological and Criminological Profile, Dublin: Department of Justice.

Partnership 2000 Expert Working Group on Childcare, 1999. National Childcare Strategy, Dublin: Stationery Office.

Peters, HE., Argys, LM., Maccoby, EE., and Mnookin, RH., 1993. "Enforcing Divorce Settlements: Evidence from Child Support Compliance and Award Modifications", Demography, 30, 719-735.

Pruett, KD., 1993, "The Paternal Presence", Families in Society: The Journal of Contemporary Human Sciences,

Quarterly National Household Survey, 2000. Second Quarter, 12 September 2000, Dublin: Central Statistics Office.

Richards, M., 1982. "Post-Divorce Arrangements for Children: A Psychological Perspective", Journal of Social Welfare Law, pp133-151.

Richardson, V., 1991. "Decision-Making by Unmarried Mothers", The Irish Journal of Psychology, Volume 12, Number 2, pp. 165-181.

Richardson, V., and Kernan, E, 1992. "The Family Life Styles of Some Single Parents in Ireland", in Kiley, G., (Editor), In and Out of Marriage: Irish and European Experiences, pp.70-86., Dublin: Family Studies Centre, University College Dublin.

Roberts, C., 1996. "The Place of Marriage in a Changing Society", Presentation to the Lord Chancellor's Conference: Supporting Marriage into the Next Century, 3 April, Working Paper Number 2, London: Family Policy Studies Centre.

Roberts, H., and MacDonald, G., 1999. "Working with Families in the Early Years", in Hill, M., (Editor), Effective Ways of Working with Children and their Families, Research Highlights in Social Work 35, London: Jessica Kingsley Publishers, Chapter Two, pp.79-69.

Robertson, S., and Williams, R., 1998. "Working with Men: A Theoretical Base for Meeting their Needs", Community Practitioner, Volume 71, Number 9, pp.286-288.

Roker, D., Richardson, H., and Coleman, J., 2000. Innovations in Parenting Support: An Evaluation of the YMCA's Parenting Teenagers Initiative, London: YMCA.

Rottman, 1994. "Allocating Money Within Households: Better Off Poorer?". In T. Nolan, and Callan, (Editors), Poverty and Policy in Ireland, Dublin: Gill and Macmillan, Chapter 13, pp.193-213.

Russell, H., and Corcoran, MP., 2000. The Experience of Those Claiming the One-Parent Family Payment, July, in Department of Social, Community and Family Affairs, Dublin: Stationery Office.

Ryce-Menuhin, J., 1996. Naked and Erect: Male Sexuality and Feeling, Illinois: Chiron Publications.

Rylands, J., 1995. A Study of Parenting Programmes in Ireland: Exploration of Needs and Current Provision, Dublin: Barnardos and the Department of Health&Children.

Schultz Jorgensen, P., 1991. "The Family with Dependent Children in Denmark", in Kiely, G. and Richardson, V., (Editors) Family Policy: European Perspectives Dublin: Family Study Centre, pp.89-104.

Second Commission on the Status of Women, 1993. Report to Government, Dublin: Stationery Office.

Sedlak, A.J. and Broadhurst, D.D., 1996. The Third National Incidence Study of Child Abuse and Neglect. Washington, DC: U.S. Department of Health and Human Services.

Seltzer, JA., 1994. "Consequences of Marital Dissolution for Children", American Review of Sociology, 20, 235-266.

Seltzer, JA., and Brandreth, Y., 1994. "What Fathers Say About Involvement with Children After Separation", Journal of Family Issues, Volume 15, Number 1, March, pp.49-77.

Seltzer, JA., 2000. "Child Support and Child Access: Experiences of Divorced and Nonmarital Families", Focus, Volume 21, Number 1, Spring, pp.54-57. Published by the Institute for Research on Poverty, University of Wisconsin-Madison, USA.

Sharry, J., Reid, P., and Donohoe, E., 2001. When Parents Separate: Helping Your Children Cope, Dublin: Veritas.

Sonenstein, FL., and Calhoun, CA., 1990. "Determinants of Child Support: A Pilot Survey of Absent Parents", Contemporary Policy Issues, 8, 75-94.

Sorensen, E., and Zibman, C., 2000. "To What Extent Do Children Benefit from Child Support? New Information from the National Survey of America's Families, 1997", Focus, Volume 21, Number 1, Spring, pp.34-37. Published by the Institute for Research on Poverty, University of Wisconsin-Madison, USA.

Speak, S., Cameron, S., and Gilroy, R., 1997. Young Single Fathers: Participation in Fatherhood – Barriers and Bridges, London: Family Policy Studies Centre.

Teachman, JD., and Paasch, KM., 1994. "Financial Impact of Divorce on Children and their Families", Future of Children, 4, pp.63-83.

The Children's Rights Alliance, 1997. Small Voices: Vital Rights – Submission to the United Nations Committee on the Rights of the Child, Dublin: The Children's Rights Alliance, 4 Christchurch Square, Dublin 8.

Thompson, E., Hanson, TL., and McLanahan, SS., 1994. "Family Structure and Child Well-Being: Economic Resources Versus Parental Behaviors", Social Forces, 73, 221-242.

United Nations Committee on the Rights of the Child, 1998. Concluding Observations on the Report Submitted by Ireland under Article 44 of the Convention, Dublin: The Children's Rights Alliance, 4 Christchurch Square, Dublin 8.

Warin, J., Solomon, Y., Lewis, C. and Langford, W., 1999. Fathers, Work and Family Life, London: Family Policy Study Centre.

Whelan C., and Fahey, T., 1994. "Marriage and the Family", in Whelan, C., (Editor), Values and Social Change in Ireland, Dublin: Gill and Macmillan, pp. 45-81.

Wilkinson, R. G., 1996. Unhealthy Societies: The Afflictions of Inequality. Routledge: London and New York.

Williams, R, 1999. Going the Distance: Fathers, Health and Health Visiting. Reading University: Professional Education in Community Studies.

Wilson, WJ., 1996. When Work Disappears: The World of the New Urban Poor, New York: Knopf.

Wilson, J., and Neckerman, K., 1986. "Poverty and Family Structure: The Widening Gap Between Evidence and Public Policy Issues", in Danzinger, S., and Weinberg, D., (Editors), Fighting Poverty, Cambridge, MA: Harvard university Press.

Working With Men, 1999. Progress Report 1999, c/o 320 Commercial Way, London SE15 1QN.